THE LOTUS
OF THE WONDERFUL LAW

THE LOTUS
OF THE WONDERFUL LAW

OR

THE LOTUS GOSPEL

SADDHARMA PUNDARĪKA SŪTRA
MIAO-FA LIEN HUA CHING

BY

W. E. SOOTHILL

CURZON
PRESS

THE LOTUS OF THE WONDERFUL LAW

Paperback edition
First published 1987 in the United Kingdom by
Curzon Press Ltd.
St John's Studios, Church Road,
Richmond Surrey TW9 2QA

ISBN 0 7007 0198 2

Reprinted 1992, 1994

In association with the
Clarendon Press at the University of Oxford

Printed and Bound in Great Britain by The Cromwell Press, Melksham, Wiltshire

PREFACE

THE Lotus Sutra of the Wonderful, or Mystic, Law is the most important religious book of the Far East. It has been described as "The Gospel of Half Asia". Dr. Timothy Richard twenty years ago translated a brief summary of its teaching, as also the profounder Śastra which he termed "The Awakening of Faith". These he published under the title of *The New Testament of Higher Buddhism*. He says: "though Buddhism has twelve different sects, yet I found the Lotus Scripture on the lecterns of every Buddhist temple I visited. It is also the chief Scripture in the Tiendai School of Buddhism in China, and is therefore the chief source of consolation to the many millions of Buddhists in the Far East." Quite recently Dr. Kenneth J. Saunders in his *The Gospel for Asia* has expressed the opinion that the three most influential religious books in the world are The Gospel of St. John, The Bhagavadgita, and The Lotus Sutra, and that what the Gospel of St. John is to the Christian and the Bhagavadgita to the Hindu, such is The Lotus to the Buddhist in the Far East. He goes farther and sees closer resemblances between the three books than others may see, at least in their ideals. When Dr. Richard published his synopsis of the Sutra under the title given above, the late Hon. Mrs. E. A. Gordon annotated it throughout with references to our New Testament with varying degrees of approximation.

Whatever view may be held of the intrinsic value of the work by Western readers, there is no doubt of its appreciation in the Far East, and it is perfectly justifiable to consider it as one of the greatest and most formative books of the world. Its influence from Tibet to Japan, from Mongolia to Cochin China has been greater than that of any other single book. For the ordinary Western reader it is much too long, as all that is said in prose is repeated in verse. There is, in consequence, repetition wearisome to the reader of many books. Undoubtedly the method of the author and of his period was useful for driving home truth to the sluggish mind, or to the mind free from other attractive entanglements. It is a method beloved of the unlettered. In order, therefore, that the Western reader may not miss the essential meaning I have omitted the repetitions and much unnecessary detail, while making it my aim to portray the message of the book as nearly as possible in its own way.

As a living book it is no longer read in Sanskrit, but only in the languages of the Far East. It is therefore their tone that I have sought to express in this abbreviated version.

The advent of Christianity to Japan has had its usual influence in arousing a moribund religion from lethargy, a lethargy which is inherent in Buddhism. A somewhat similar revival with a similar cause is occurring in China. In consequence, a fresh interest has arisen in Buddhist literature and not least in The Lotus. For this reason in 1921 I wrote to China for a copy of the Chinese text. Though the pages are less peppered with Sanskrit transliterations and Buddhist terms than other Buddhist classics, the work still presents serious difficulty to the Chinese reader and not less so to the Western student. It was therefore my purpose to translate the text for the use of the Western student.

The books had scarcely arrived in Oxford when one of those curious coincidences occurred, which the devout ascribe to external intervention, be it by the Buddha, as my visitor thought, or by some other Spiritual Power. An unusual type of visitor called on me. His name was Bunno Kato. It transpired that he was a Japanese leader of the Nichiren School of Buddhism. Most modestly he preferred of me an earnest request, that I would help him in translating into English The Lotus scripture. It is the great text of his School as also of certain other Schools of Buddhism. He knew the lengthy text by heart, and was intimately acquainted with the voluminous commentaries written on the work. The Chinese text common to Japan and China is the Kumarajiva version made in A.D. 406. It was with pleasure that we began our work on it together. A more faithful, or intelligent devotee of the work could not have been found. After nearly four years of application the English translation was finished in 1925. My final revision was completed at Harbin in Manchuria, while waiting for the Trans-Siberian train to bring me home after a visit to China, where I had gone as a member of Lord Willingdon's Commission. I was anxious to send the final corrections to Mr. Kato via

China, for any papers carried through Russia were suspect and liable to confiscation, as I proved on my way through.

The translation of the whole work is still in manuscript, along with Mr. Kato's extensive introduction. It will form too large a book to appeal to any but students of the subject. I am therefore taking this method of making the work better known to the general reader of the Western world.

Too long has this literary masterpiece been buried in translations, unavoidably cumbrous and inspirationally innocuous. Hence this endeavour to reveal the contour of the most powerful spiritual drama known in the Far East.

W. E. S.

CONTENTS

LIST OF ILLUSTRATIONS

Acknowledgement for permission to use the above illustrations is gratefully made to the British Museum and Dr. Lionel Giles for Nos. 1, 9, and 12; to Lady Hosie for No. 2, and to the Bodleian Library for the other illustrations, which are taken from the eighteenth-century woodcuts of the 釋迦如來應化事蹟, *Shih-chia Ju-lai Ying-hua Shih-chi, or Scenes from the Life of the Buddha.*

In this new impression the Frontispiece and illustration number 2 have been omitted for technical reasons.

INTRODUCTION

Historical

By whom was this classic given? Devout Buddhists in the Far East say it contains the very words of Sakyamuni, the Buddha, his final teaching spoken towards the end of his days on the Vulture Peak in Nepal. Equally devout Buddhists in Ceylon, Burma, and Siam declare that it was entirely unknown in the ancient Canon, that it contradicts the essential teaching of the Buddha, and that it is the invention of a much later age. Thus we see Buddhism separated into its two great divisions, and it is over the works, of which The Lotus is the most representative type, that the division of Hinayana and Mahayana arises. These two terms were invented by the Mahayanists, who form the "Northern" School of Buddhism, that is the Far Eastern School now found in China, Japan, Korea, Mongolia, Tibet. The Hinayanists are the "Southern", or Orthodox, School of Ceylon, Burma, Siam. Hinayana means Small wain, or vehicle; Mahayana, Large wain, or vehicle. By the Northern Buddhist, Hinayana is charged with conveying only the few to Nirvana, that is, those seeking salvation by the arduous way of works. Mahayana, on the other hand, professes to open the way for the many, indeed finally for all. Consequently Mahayanism is another term for Universalism, or Catholicism.

In Mahayana, salvation is attained not by laborious

effort, but simply by faith in the Buddhas and Bodhisattvas. The great Bodhisattvas in particular are objects of faith and invocation. They are not historical beings but idealizations. Accredited with a vow not to enter into the final bliss of Buddhahood until all creatures are saved, they instantly respond to all who call upon them. Their salvation is not to a Nirvana of individual extinction or annihilation, but to heavens of joy and blessedness. Such happiness is infinite, to which all will finally attain. Those who claim it now by faith and invocation will escape the perils and pains of reincarnation. Those who delay their belief will continue to suffer until they cry for salvation, as they ultimately will cry.

Here lies the contrast, the difference, between the one School and the other—a difference at least as fundamental as between Roman and Reformed Christianity. But Roman and Reformed virtually make appeal to the same Book, or collection of books, the Bible. Not so is it with Hinayana and Mahayana, for they appeal to two differing sets of textual authorities. Hinayanists claim, with a measure of justice, that their texts are the only ancient and valid canons, and that these alone contain the real teaching of their Founder. Mahayanists, it is true, claim all those texts equally with their rivals, but declare that they were only the Buddha's preparatory teaching, suited to the immature degree of his disciples' immediate development. They insist that their Mahayana texts were his developed doctrine, given towards the end of his ministry, when his disciples were mature enough to understand his spiritual interpretation of the universe and of universal truth. They say that his attitude, during the period of Hinayana texts, was similar to the attitude of the schoolmaster, who leads on his pupils according to their ability through the preparatory stages, but when they are sufficiently grounded reveals to them the higher learning. Consequently they claim that the Buddha only in the later stages of his life and before his departure, made the full revelation. This perfect revelation, they assert, is only to be found in the Mahayana texts; it is a revelation of the "All-Truth" which his disciples had been trained by easy stages finally to apprehend in its fullness.

The detached mind will not easily be beguiled into acceptance of the Mahayanist's special pleading. Mahayanists have not a shred of real evidence to show that the Buddha ever delivered any of the addresses attributed by them to him. All the weight of evidence is indeed against them. Whatever evidence there is rather supports the Hinayanists' claim to Apostolic Succession. Though these may not possess documentary evidence of the Buddha's actual sermons, at least the Sutras of Southern Buddhism may be considered as in the direct line of his teaching. As to the Mahayana Sutras, the unprejudiced cannot doubt that they are the invention of a later period, and that Mahayanism is a shoot grafted on to the original stock of the Buddhist Bodhi-tree. Whence, where and when this scion was grafted is still unknown. There are able scholars who assert that there is no need to look abroad for Mahayana ideas, because their embryo can be discovered in the orthodox scriptures. But there seems more justification for supposing the new scion to be of external origin, grafted on to Buddhism, perhaps in Northern India, perhaps still farther north in Central Asia. Whatever its origin this scion, grafted into the old tree, produced fruit of a different quality, more attractive to the eye and the taste; it was this off-shoot that struck in the north and east of Asia. The original stock grew older, died in its native soil, and was only saved by a branch which had been transplanted away from its native hills with their wintry snows to the southern sun, where it survives.

We may say, then, that The Lotus never had any direct connexion with Śakyamuni. It was the brilliant concept of a later age. The author, whose name and place of origin are unknown, was one of the world's greatest Apocalyptists. He was gifted with a rare imagination, and with remarkable dramatic powers which appeal to an imaginative and florid race. He was endowed with talents of detail and repetition that, while tedious and often puerile to our sated taste, were of prime value in capturing the attention of his readers and in impressing his story on a leisurely people. His brilliant drama of spiritual things has outshone his name, while unconsciously he has been one of the chief instruments in dividing Buddhism. The inspiration that was to weld a fracture already yawning split it permanently in two. The two segments remain apart. The Southern Buddhists

4

of Burma, Ceylon, Siam guard the treasure of the earthly Buddha's law, as they now guard the coffin supposed to contain his earthly remains so recently recovered. The Northern or Far Eastern Buddhists guard the treasure of an Eternal Buddha, of whom the earthly Buddha was but a temporal manifestation. Thus does Mahayana, or the universal chariot of salvation, compare itself with the Southern Hinayana, or the small chariot of laborious "works", which saves the few. In reality Mahayanism is, as the Southern Buddhists believe, a betrayal of Śakyamuni Buddha, in the interests of doctrines he never taught and which are a reversal of his principles, as recorded by his disciples.

As to the author, not only is his name unknown, but even the region of his origin is equally obscure. Presumably the writer composed the work in Sanskrit and in Northern India; it may, however, have been composed farther north in Central Asia. Though its date or period is not discovered, it seems to have been both a product, and perhaps a producer, of the re-action against the formalism which had fallen upon ascetic Buddhism.

Was it the offspring of ideas which had already hailed the dawn of spiritual liberation across Western Asia? That is a question to which as yet there is no sufficient answer. Whatever the answer may be we now know that Buddhism, at the beginning of the Christian era, was a potent religious force across Central Asia, that its missionaries had already reached Western China and that, during the first century of

5

our era, the religion, in a form clearly not of the Mahayana order, was welcomed at the Imperial Chinese Court. The Scythian ruler of Northern India, Kanishka, gave it his ardent support during that century, as the ruler Aśoka had done centuries earlier. That the Buddhism of Kanishka's period differed from the original cult is probable, but we do not yet know in what respect.

It must not be assumed that the new doctrines of salvation, which found their expression in the tractate "The Uprising (Awakening) of Faith" and in "The Lotus Sutra", were necessarily created by these works. It is more likely that those doctrines only found their ultimate expression in these works. Nor can we assume that they were known before Christian influence was felt in the lands of the new Buddhism. Though by no means convinced, or concerned, that Christian influence had anything to do with the creation of the new cult, yet I cannot ignore the fact that the first assured appearance in China of The Lotus was towards the end of the third century A.D. The Christian Church in India, whose foundation is attributed to the Apostle Thomas, may or may not have existed. That is perhaps a matter of minor importance to our subject in comparison with an influence of recognized potency, namely, the interchange of ideas which spread east and west along the remarkable trading corridor that stretched from Northern China to the Mediterranean. Graeco-Bactrian art is an instance of such propagation. Whether this uprising of the human spirit was a natural protest against

6

priestcraft and ritual, is a question more easily put than answered. Here I can only call attention to the undoubted interchange of such ideas as existing before and after the Christian era.

We are on surer ground when we seek to trace the story of the translation of The Lotus into Chinese. The first partial version, of which no copy exists, was made by an unknown author in or about A.D. 255–6. Another lost version in twenty-eight chapters was made in A.D. 265, by the monk Dharmaraksha. He, or another of the same name, apparently made another version in A.D. 286 which still exists. A fourth version, now lost, was made by a translator of unknown origin in A.D. 335. The fifth version, which holds the field, is that from which the present excerpts are made. Its literary quality shows that it could only have been composed by very scholarly Chinese. But the actual translator to the Chinese pundits was Kumarajiva and he completed the work in A.D. 406. Kumarajiva is said to have come to China, or as some say was captured and brought there, from Kharashar in Turkestan. Others describe him as of "Takchas'ila" (Taxila) in the neighbourhood of Chitral. From A.D. 397 to 415 he lived in the Ch'in capital of Ch'ang-an in modern Shensi. At that time China was in a state of partition. Yao Hsing, the Ch'in ruler, supported and encouraged Kumarajiva, providing him with a large staff of Chinese writers for his very numerous translations and works.

A sixth version, still existing, was made in A.D. 601 by Jñanagupta and Dharmagupta, two monks

7

reputed to be of Indian origin, and it agrees with the Sanskrit version in having twenty-seven chapters. The verses in Chapter XXV of Kumarajiva's version were not made by him but by a Jñanagupta of the Northern Chou dynasty A.D. 557–89; whether it was the same monk is not clear.

The three existing versions then are the Dharmaraksha version of A.D. 286, that of Kumarajiva which agrees with the Tibetan version, and that of Jñanagupta. Little is known of the sources whence these versions were made. Jñanagupta says that he has seen two originals, one on palm-leaves, the other on a silk-like fabric, which differed considerably from each other. Dharmaraksha's version he says was from that on palm-leaves, Kumarajiva's from the fabric. The palm-leaf version seems to have been in Sanskrit; the fabric version was in Kharashar characters, the writing used in Kuche (Kwei-tz), the supposed native place of Kumarajiva. The Kharashar text used by him is said to have been older than that on the palm-leaves.

We possess, then, a version by Kumarajiva which is accepted in the Far East. The Chinese date for its translation, A.D. 406, may be accepted, for its extraordinary popularity over a thousand years ago is attested by the large number of portions brought from the Tun Huang monastery by Sir Aurel Stein and now in the British Museum. These copies, made between A.D. 533 and 972, as also an earlier commentary of A.D. 508, lay hidden in a walled-up chamber probably from the eleventh century until the present century. The discovery and the bringing

8

1. End of a roll of Chapter X of the Lotus Sutra in the Stein Collection at the British Museum

It was written on paper on May 4th, A.D. 533, six centuries before paper was made in Europe. The roll was found, with many others, by Sir Aurel M. Stein, in the Cave of the Thousand Buddhas at Tun-huang. The photograph shows the last five lines of the text, the name of the Sutra, chapter, date, and name and description of the writer

of these copies to the light of the world is one of the romances of our generation. Sir Aurel, on his second intrepid journey of discovery from Kashmir to Kansu, followed the route taken by the famous Chinese monk Hsüan (or Yüan) Tsang, who in the seventh century made a pilgrimage from China to India. After crossing the dread Taklamakan desert, he reached Tun Huang in Kansu. In the cave-temple of The Thousand Buddhas the abbot in charge,.while making repairs, had broken into a closed-up room, whose existence was till then unknown, where he found hidden a great collection of written scrolls. Sir Aurel, after much difficulty, secured a selection of the scrolls, and amongst them were the numerous portions of The Lotus Sutra already mentioned.

From the Sanskrit versions previously brought to the west during the nineteenth century two translations were made, one into French, the other into English. The French version, made from a manuscript provided by Mr. Brian Hodgson, was completed by Eugène Burnouf in 1852 under the title *Le Lotus de la bonne loi*. The English version was made by H. Kern of Leiden in 1909; it was published, under the title *Saddharma Pundarika*, as vol. xxi of the Sacred Books of the East. Both these translations were made for scholars.

As yet no translation of the Chinese version has been published, yet it is the Chinese version which is most in use in the Far East. There indeed The Lotus Sutra has its home; to many of the sects of "Northern Buddhism" it is a fundamental work, and

9

by all it is highly valued. To "Southern Buddhists" it is, as already stated, heterodox and contrary to the teaching of their founder Śakyamuni. The complete text has now been translated into English by Mr. Kato and myself and it is hoped will yet be available to the Western student of Buddhism. It will be of value to those who wish to read in its entirety one of the oldest and most popular works giving the fully developed Mahayana doctrine. Nor will it be less useful to many who desire a work replete with Buddhist terminology which, translated phrase by phrase, can easily be compared with the Chinese text.

The Kumarajiva version, on which the present synopsis is based, is especially remarkable for the skill shown by the Chinese scholars in rendering his oral translations into their own written language. His version is probably more a paraphrase than a literal translation, but in the absence of the original text it is difficult to speak with assurance. However that may be, the Chinese scholars produced under him a work of great literary merit. The form of construction is strict and difficult, and the skill shown in the prose is as great as in the poetic part. A more gifted pen may yet reproduce the measure in English where my efforts have failed. Such failure has at least emphasized my opinion that Kumarajiva's Chinese version is one of the world's literary masterpieces.

Form and Content

In Kumarajiva's version, as in Dharmaraksha's previous translation, there are twenty-eight chapters.

In the Sanskrit version and in Jñanagupta's Chinese translation there are twenty-seven. The difference is brought about in Chapter XI of the Sanskrit, which is given in two parts by the two first-named translators, making Chapters XI and XII.

From the first to the twenty-first chapters of Kumarajiva's version almost everything is said first in prose then in verse. The same remark applies to the corresponding chapters in the Sanskrit. The remaining chapters in both are without the verse repetition, with the noticeable exception of the twenty-fifth chapter on Avalokitesvara, i. e. Kwan-yin or Kwannon which, both in the Chinese and the Sanskrit versions, has prose and verse.

Each section, prose and verse, would, if separated, make a fairly complete whole. Whether the verse section, the gathas, preceded the prose is a question that Sanskrit scholars have not yet decided. Linguistic differences suggest that the drama was first composed in verse, and that the prose section was introduced later. The question can only be decided by those competent to judge. At present we must accept the version as it stands. The verse part in general follows the tenor of the prose discourse, but the differences are many. All the prose sections in Chinese are done into short sentences of similar length, which can be read rhythmically. All the verse parts differ in form from the Sanskrit, being in lines of sometimes four, sometimes five monosyllabic words to the line. In the translation here offered no attempt has been made to recast the order of the prose

II

sentences or the verse lines; for with rare exceptions it has proved possible to translate them phrase by phrase, or line by line, thus providing the reader with a translation conveying the structure of the original in its presentation of ideas. No language not mono-syllabic could possibly portray the form.

The following quotation from Chapter II may be taken as an example of the verse rhythm, if read as a four-beat measure:

> " List well to the Law
> Obtained by the Buddhas,
> Which by infinite tact
> They expound to the living,
> Whose inmost thoughts,
> The ways they tread,
> Their desires diverse,
> Their former karmas,
> The Buddha knows well.
> Hence with reason and parable,
> Terms and expedients,
> He leads all to rejoice,
> Telling them sutras,
> Or poems, or stories,
> Or marvels, or reasonings.
>
> To some I preach Nirvana,
> An expedient to lead them
> To enter Buddha-wisdom,
> But to these I'd not yet said
> 'You all shall become buddhas',
> For the time had not arrived."

From the first chapter we find The Lotus Sutra to be unique in the world of religious literature. A magnificent apocalyptic, it presents a spiritual drama of the highest order, with the universe as its stage, eternity as its period, and Buddhas, gods, men, devils, as the dramatis personae. From the most distant worlds and from past aeons, the eternal Buddhas throng the stage to hear the mighty Buddha proclaim his ancient and eternal Truth. Bodhisattvas flock to his feet; gods from the heavens, men from all quarters of the earth, the tortured from the deepest hells, the demons themselves crowd to hear the tones of the Glorious One.

Though the divine Speaker is the Buddha, even the earthly Śakyamuni Buddha, no longer is he the human Buddha, but the Eternal One. On earth he had assumed the human form with all its limitations. Now he reveals himself, *sub specie aeternitatis*, as the Eternal, Omniscient, Omnipotent, Omnipresent Buddha, creator-destroyer, recreator of all worlds, every world a Lotus rising from the waters to flower, shed its fragrance and die, only that fresh flowers may eternally spring.

The scene opens with the Buddha seated on Mount Gridhrakuta, or the Vulture Peak, in Nepal. Here the mount on which he had taught is spiritualized. Around him are gathered his 12,000 purified disciples, thousands more who had not yet completed their course, 80,000 bodhisattvas, 60,000 devas or gods, Brahma and his following of 12,000, dragon-kings with their hundreds of thousands, and demon

13

kings with hundreds of thousands of followers. There, to all these orders of living beings, the Buddha displays the meaning of the Infinite, while from heaven there rain down countless showers of superb flowers filling the air with their fragrance, and all the universe is shaken.

From the centre of his forehead the Buddha sends forth a ray of light which lights up 18,000 worlds to the east, upwards to their highest heavens, downwards to their lowest hells. In like manner he shines upon and reveals the worlds in the other quarters, with all their living beings. In every world is revealed a Buddha teaching vast congregations of disciples.

Thus does the Buddha reveal his infinite worlds in infinite time. It is a colossal conception, expressed with an art that appeals to all who can enter into the spirit of the drama and allow the mind to imagine so tremendous a scene.

In the second act, Chapter II, the Buddha is presented coming forth from a trance-like meditation to explain why he had heretofore confined his teaching to the narrower way of works, while now he makes the greater revelation of faith. As a wise master he had been compelled to follow the tactical method of expediency, because his disciples could not receive the higher wisdom, the more brilliant light, except by previous preparation. Only a Buddha, an Enlightened One, can fathom the meaning of All Existence, and his disciples, in their lower stage of wisdom, would never have been able to believe it possible that they also were called to Buddhahood, to the fullest enlightenment of the Buddha himself. Hence he had to lead them on by measured steps. Even now his All-truth is so vast that he fears to express it lest "all the worlds of gods, men, and demons be startled and perplexed and the doubting amongst his disciples fall into the great pit". So portentous is the air, and so filled with doubt and foreboding are the hearts of his hearers, that multitudes withdraw, unable to bear the announcement which is to shatter all their past hardly-acquired merits. Here we trace an indication of the breach between the Hinayanists who withdraw and the Mahayanists who remain. At last only the host of faithful bodhisattvas remain, and to them he declares that none but they have power to apprehend his mystery. He proceeds to tell them that though he has seemed to preach other vehicles or modes of salvation, essentially there is but One Vehicle. The other yana have been but temporary expedients. There is but the One Vehicle, that in which the Buddha himself abides, and with which he will save all creatures, bringing them to the true Nirvana, which is not extinction of existence but extinction of all ills and all ignorance. All who pay homage to the Buddha, if with but a simple flower, are thereby admitted to the fellowship of countless Buddhas. Not one will fail to become Buddha, for all Buddhas have vowed to save all beings to perfect enlightenment, that is to perfect Buddhahood.

In the third chapter comes the joyous response of Sariputra, full of ecstasy at the assurance that he is now "really a son of Buddha, born from the mouth of Buddha", freed from all his errors and doubts and already possessed of the real Nirvana, the extinction of all ills, filled with a sublime peace. The Buddha responds telling him that in his later development he will be called Flower-Light Buddha, that he will reign over a world called Undefiled, and that wherever the feet of his disciples tread jewel-flowers will spring. Soon follows the Parable of the Burning House which is given in this volume. Śariputra, wishing to share his joy with his 1,200 brethren, asks what is to be their lot.

The answer is withheld for a time, or perhaps expressed in the form of parables; for instance, in Chapter IV occurs the Parable of the Prodigal Son, or the Seeking Father, the Buddha being the Father who seeks his wandering son and at last finds him and endows him with all his wealth. Again, in Chapter V, is the Parable of the Trees and Herbs, on which the Buddha, like a great cloud, pours his rain without discrimination or stint; fertilizing each according to its need and receptivity. After this interlude he proceeds to predict in Chapter VI the future of his disciples; for instance, he foretells that Maha-Kaśyapa will be the Buddha Radiance, his Buddha-world being known as Radiant Virtue and his Buddha-period named Great Magnificence; that Subhuti will be the Buddha Name-Form in a Realm of Jewels, in a Buddha-period Jewel-kalpa; another's Buddha-name will be Golden-Light, and another's Fragrance of Sandal-wood. Then comes a further artistic interlude in the

16

Parable of the Magic City on the weary way to the
Land of Jewels, which forms the title and one of the
subjects of Chapter VII. This parable follows on
the marvellous story of a Buddha who, in his human
existence, had sixteen sons, all of whom became
Buddhas and preached in their generation the wonderful Lotus doctrine. In Chapter VIII the Buddha
returns to the prediction of the future of his disciples,
when five hundred of them learn their fate, as do
others. The prediction is continued in Chapter IX
when it is extended to other multitudes. There are
parallels with the Revelation of St. John in that each
receives a new name and dwells in a realm with a new
name.

Chapter X is called The Preacher and contains an
address to the Lord of Healing, or King of Medicine,
in which the exceeding value of the Lotus Sutra is
declared. So valuable indeed is it that if any one hear
a single verse, or a single word of it, and by a single
thought delight in it, their perfect enlightenment is
assured. Any one who recites one verse only of the
Sutra, or offers incense to it, or merely bows before
it, foretells thereby his early escape from the realm
of men and his translation to buddhahood. On the
other hand, though all other blasphemy, even of the
Buddha, may be considered light, he who blasphemes
the Sutra with a single word, or abuses one reciting
it, is guilty of what the Christian would term the sin
against the Holy Ghost. On the contrary, he who
recites the Sutra is thereby clad in the Buddha's
mantle and adorns himself with the Buddha's adorn-

ment; such a one is worthy of the highest reverence and of the richest gifts; for the Lotus is the secret and mystic doctrine of the Buddha.

It is in Chapter XI that the drama reaches the supreme moment of its presentation. A great stupa or shrine, superbly decorated, appears in the sky, whose light and fragrance and music fill the whole earth. Gods and spirits rain flowers and perfumes upon it. From its midst comes a great voice: World-honoured Śakyamuni! Thou art able to preach to the great assembly the Wonderful Law-flower Sutra of universal and mighty Wisdom, which none but bodhisattvas can learn, and which the Buddhas keep under their own guardianship. What thou proclaimest is the Truth.

The vast multitude of disciples pray eagerly that the Occupant of this heavenly shrine may be revealed to them. They are told that he who is within is The Ancient Buddha, or as we might perhaps say, The Ancient of Days, whose name means Many Precious things, or Abundant Treasures. Infinite ages ago he had vowed that whenever in any world the Lotus was first proclaimed, there would he be in the midst. Only, if he were to reveal himself, it must be in the presence of the countless host of Buddhas who were the off-spring of the Buddha he came to hear. Thereupon Śakyamuni sends forth from between his eyebrows the sacred ray of light, which illuminates all his Buddha-worlds first to the east, then to the south, west, and north, the zenith and nadir. In each direction all the Buddhas and bodhisattvas are revealed preaching to

18

their countless hosts of disciples with ravishing voices, under jewelled canopies. The ray of light is recognized at once as the summons to attend upon the shrine of the Ancient Buddha, and hear that marvel of marvels the preaching of The Lotus. With all their vast trains they come joyfully from east and west, from north and south, from zenith and nadir, each taking up his station in the sky, seated on his lion-throne under his allotted jewel-tree. A gorgeous picture of a Celestial Durbar is thus displayed. Filled is the sky with a countless celestial host, when Śakyamuni Buddha approaches the shrine and with a sound as of thunder withdraws its bolt. The doors swing open to reveal on a lion throne the undissipated body of the Ancient Buddha, living and seated in deepest meditation. Lifting up his voice he announces that he has come, according to his age-long vow, to hear The Lotus proclaimed by Śakyamuni. To this end he beckons him to enter the shrine and share his lion-throne. Such is the Revelation of the Ancient Buddha, not as dead but as living.

Beholding all this marvel while still on the earth, the disciples of Śakyamuni now implore that they too no longer be tied to earth, but be received up to join the celestial host. Thereupon Śakyamuni, by his transcendent power, raises the whole company of his disciples into the sky and with a great voice cries: "Who is able to proclaim the Wonderful Law-Flower Sutra in this Saha-world? Now indeed is the time. The Tathagata (Buddha) must himself speedily enter Nirvana, but wills to bequeath this wonderful Sutra

19

so that it may ever live in the world." Therefore he calls on all present to take the great Mahayana vow.

With Chapter XII begins the difference between those versions with twenty-seven chapters and those with twenty-eight.

In the Sanskrit version our Chapter XII is the latter half of Chapter XI. Though generally considered to be part of the original text, it bears the impress of an interpolation, for the next chapter, (our Chapter XIII) follows naturally on the call just made to take the Mahayana vow. It is said that Kumarajiva omitted this part from his Chinese version, or, if he included it, that for a time it was omitted from the copies made. The hermit referred to in the opening incident of our Chapter XII is named, in the verse section, Asita. Now it is recorded that after the birth of Gautama a certain saint Asita took the infant into his arms, as Simeon did the child Jesus in the Gospel, and foretold his destiny. The chapter is styled Devadatta. This was the name of the cousin and rival of Sakyamuni Buddha, whom he is accused of trying to kill, for which it is reported he was swallowed up in hell. Nevertheless there was a sect which worshipped him as a Buddha up to A.D. 400, but his story is unreliable. By some he is said to be a reincarnation of Asita, which naturally is beyond proof. Here the Buddha is made to announce that it was Devadatta who had taught him The Lotus Sutra. The devout consider this chapter to prove that even a wicked creature like Devadatta, though doomed to hell for trying to kill the Buddha, may still be converted and become Buddha.

The chapter opens by Śakyamuni recounting that, in a former incarnation when he was a king, he devoted himself to a tireless search for the Supreme Wisdom. During long kalpas he gave alms of every kind with the utmost self-sacrifice. At last he, the king, offered to become the menial follower of any one who would reveal to him the Truth. Then it was that the hermit Devadatta called him to be his disciple, promising to teach him The Lotus Truth. He responded with joy and became his servant, for love of the wonderful truth revealed by the hermit. Śakyamuni now foretells the glorious future of Devadatta.

Soon, one of the attendants on the Ancient Buddha from a lower region, evidently a-weary, invites his master to dismiss the durbar and return home. On this Śakyamuni intervenes, requesting the attendant to await the arrival of Manjuśri who will tell of the marvellous effect of The Lotus Sutra during his preaching of it. Manjuśri arrives on a thousand-petal lotus flower and, after paying his homage to the two Buddhas, tells the story of his adventures in the Dragon Palace of the sea, where, in the deep, he has converted infinite numbers. At his call myriads of bodhisattvas arise from the ocean and are assembled on the mountain side seated on jewelled lotuses, after which they ascend into the sky to join the great multitude. Later a greater marvel occurs, for the daughter of the Dragon-king attains to The Lotus wisdom and thereby is instantly changed into a young man. It amazes the assembly for "the body of a woman is filthy and not a vessel of the Law", whereas here, by immediate conversion, a female can enter into all the privileges of the man, even to that of becoming a king, a Brahma, a Buddha. The moral is easy to draw, that The Lotus doctrine knows no distinction of male or female, but that even a woman may enter into the fullness of Anuttara-samyak-sambodhi, or Perfect Enlightenment.

In Chapter XIII the Lord of Healing bids Śakyamuni Buddha, who is going to his Nirvana, not to have any anxiety, for he and his twenty thousand Bodhisattvas now take a vow to make The Lotus Sutra their charge. During the evil age to come they will faithfully preach it to all creatures, unsparing of body or life. Other countless followers of the Buddha take a like vow. Then the Buddha's aunt, his foster-mother, leading her six thousand nuns, stands before him, looking sadly on his face. Realizing that they think they have been overlooked, he asks them why they have not understood? Has he not promised perfect enlightenment to *all* his disciples, and does not this include them? Then he promises that they also will in turn become Buddhas. His foster-mother will become a Buddha called Loveliness, and all her disciples will become perfectly enlightened. His wife, the mother of his son Rahula, he foretells will become a Buddha entitled The Perfect One of the Myriad Rays. All the women thereupon vow to preach The Lotus Sutra in all lands. Following this, the countless number of spiritual bodhisattvas, as with a lion's roar, vow to preach the Sutra in all worlds in every direction.

The following Chapter XIV, called "A Serene Life", is an instruction how the vow is to be kept. Rules of life for the disciple are laid down in considerable detail. His virtues are patience, gentleness, a mind unperturbed, seeing all things in their reality, or, as we might say fluid, or spiritual. There must be no intimacy with kings and rulers as such, nor with heretics, nor with authors of worldly literature or poetry, nor with players, boxers and jugglers, nor with butchers, hunters or fishermen, nor with women; he may preach to them, but have no intimacy with them of any kind. To all and in all circumstances he must show charity. Let him fear not staves nor swords, for he will be divinely protected on every hand. Then follows the parable of the king, who rewards his faithful soldiers with all his possessions, save only the lustrous jewel he wears on his brow. At last even this he cannot keep for himself but bestows it also. Thus is it with the Buddha and his priceless jewel The Lotus.

"Springing up out of the Earth" is the title of the next, the fifteenth chapter. The host of Bodhisattvas from other realms offer to Śakyamuni to remain in his realm and preach the Sutra. No need, is his reply, and from the earth spring vast, countless numbers of bodhisattvas, each of them leading forth disciples many as the sands of Ganges, who all make obeisance to the two Buddhas, the Ancient One and Śakyamuni, and walk in procession round them. Fifty kalpas, or myriads of years pass while thus they march, though it seems but as half a day. Whence came they? ask the disciples. Then the Buddha calls forth Maitreya, who is the Buddha-to-come, and to him announces that these are the disciples he has taught through vast ages, who now dwell in a vast realm below the earth in the Space-region of the world. But, how is it possible that Śakyamuni in so short a lifetime can have taught such a vast multitude? ask the disciples astonished. Through Maitreya they express their doubt while depicting in detail the brief life and period of Śakyamuni.

This leads in Chapter XVI to the climax of the drama, where he reveals that his life is hemmed in by no bounds of time and space, for he is eternal. The chapter is called The Revelation of the Buddha as Eternal. "Since I veritably was Buddha, infinite, boundless, hundreds, thousands, myriads, kotis, nayutas of kalpas have passed." With much illustration, as will be found in this volume, he tries to explain the incalculable meaning of eternity and claims that he has always been Buddha. He describes his eternal being, his omniscience and his omnipresence. He tells them he must leave them for their own good, because even a Buddha may only appear at rare intervals, for familiarity breeds contempt, even for a Buddha. All this he shows in the Parable of the Good Physician, whose sons drink poison and refuse his remedies till he temporarily departs and leaves them.

In the next Chapter XVII, he tells Maitreya that, during the time that he has been proclaiming the Eternity of his Life, beings countless as the sands of

Ganges have been saved, and numberless others attained enhanced powers. Flowers, incense, jewels rain down from heaven upon the two Buddhas in the heavenly shrine, while all the Bodhisattvas sing countless praises with heavenly voices. Vast and eternal are the rewards promised to the true believer, all expressed with a wealth of detail impossible to repeat here.

In Chapter XVIII, called The Merits of Joyful Accordance, the Buddha recounts still further the reward that will follow the merit of believing in The Lotus Sutra. Other merits of untold value are discussed, but the merit of faith in The Lotus surpasses all these myriad-fold. On earth the believer will be free from every ailment, for instance, "his teeth will never be dirty, black or yellow, nor in gaps, nor fall out, nor be irregular, nor crooked, his lips will not be pendulous, nor twisted and shrunk, nor coarse and rough, nor have sores and pustules, nor be cracked and broken, nor awry and out of shape, neither thick nor big, neither sallow nor black, having nothing loathsome; his nose will not be flat, nor crooked and distorted," and so on in further detail. Hereafter he will be born among gods or men, possessing elephants, horses and carriages, jewelled palanquins and litters, and every other luxury.

Further rewards are promised in Chapter XIX—rewards for merits of eye, of ear, of nose, of tongue, of body and of mind, all which are separately described. With his ear he will hear the sounds of his entire universe, from its highest heaven to its lowest hell, the sounds of elephants, horses, oxen, carriages, wailing, lamentation, conches, drums, gongs, bells, laughter, speech, men, women, boys, girls, the lawful, the unlawful, pain, pleasure, and so on, the sounds of its Bodhisattvas and Buddhas being included. In like manner are the other organs presented in un-stinted detail.

This is followed by Chapter XX on the Bodhisattva "Never despise". Wherever he met a person, good or bad, he always addressed him with reverence, as one whose final destiny was buddhahood. Ignorant of everything else, and always repeating "You are to become buddhas", he stirred people to anger. They beat him severely, while he still saluted them and told them they were destined to buddhahood. As he drew near the end of his normal term of life, he acquired control over the six organs referred to in the last chapter and became possessed of the rewards attached thereto. So influential did he become that all those who had despised and beaten him, chief among whom were his fellow-monks and nuns, became his dis-ciples. After his translation he entered the company of myriads of Buddhas in Light. Then the Buddha, after telling this story, says, I myself was that Buddha "Never Despise." The persecuting monks are, of course, those of the Hinayana, the persecuted those of the Mahayana.

In Chapter XXI the "Divine Power of the Buddha is revealed". The method of the revelation of power is startling and far from attractive to the Western mind, but it indicates the value of lingual enlightenment. All living beings in all the universes now assemble together before the Celestial Shrine, and flowers, incense, garlands, canopies, jewels, and every precious thing fill the sky like gathering clouds, being transformed into a mighty jewel-canopy above the Buddhas. Śakyamuni again addresses the gathered host in praise of this Sutra, which he declares contains all the law of the Buddha, all his sovereign powers, all the mystery of his treasury.

"The Final Commission" is the title of Chapter XXII. Śakyamuni by supernatural power places his hand on the heads of the countless Bodhisattvas present, entrusting to them The Lotus law of Perfect Enlightenment. The Tathagata is described as the Great Lord of Giving and they in like manner must give this Sutra to all. Thereupon Śakyamuni dismisses all the Buddhas from all the other Buddharealms: "Buddhas! Peace be unto you. Let the stupa of the Buddha, Abundant Treasures, be restored as before." On this all depart rejoicing greatly that they have heard the preaching of Śakyamuni.

It seems probable that the author here ended his drama, though it is noteworthy that this chapter is not done into verse and that, with the exception of Chapter XXV, no further verse portion is found. Nothing is said about the entry of Śakyamuni into his Nirvana, but that may be an artistic and intentional omission. Six more chapters follow, by which presumably some later writer or writers thought to improve the work. They serve no such purpose, and Buddhism would lose nothing by their omission

That they formed part of the work as it reached China need not be doubted, but the dismissal of the Celestial Assembly seems the natural conclusion for a work revealing such dramatic skill and power.

It may be added that this Chapter XXII is not, in the Sanskrit version, found here, but as the final chapter, and also in Jñanagupta's Chinese translation. In Dharmaraksha's version, Chapter XXV on Avalokiteśvara, or Kuan-yin, precedes it. This may be an indication of the position already gained in the third century A.D. by Kuan-yin, the Regarder of Cries. The remaining chapters are, however, clearly *hors d'œuvre*, and spoil the drama. Whether it was for this reason that Kumarajiva placed the Final Commission here, or whether such was its position in the text he used, can at present only be matter of conjecture. In the Sanskrit version our Chapters XXIII to XXVIII are interpolated, or so it would appear, the present chapter being put last. That Chapters XXIII to XXVIII have been considered as additions seems also evident from the different order in which they appear. Kern points out that the Sanskrit and Jñanagupta's versions take as their order our Chapters XXVI, XXIII, XXIV, XXV, XXVII, XXVIII, and XXII; while Dharmaraksha's order is our Chapters XXV, XXII, XXIII, XXIV, XXVI, XXVII, and XXVIII.

Assuming then, what is doubtful, that our Chapter XXII is the final chapter of the original apocalypse, and that the remaining six are by later writers, though as early as the third century A.D., we find in Chapter

28

XXIII "The Story of the Bodhisattva King of Healing". It may be noted that sickness and religious healing are closely associated in Buddhism. The King of the Constellation-flower asks Śakyamuni-Buddha why the King of Healing wanders through, and suffers in this universe, healing countless diseases. The Buddha in reply tells him that, in ages gone by, there was a Buddha called Brilliance of the Sun and Moon, who finally preached The Lotus Truth to one of his numberless Bodhisattvas called Beautiful. Beautiful thereupon entered into the samadhi known as the Revelation of all forms, or things. In thank-offering he resolved to offer up his body to Buddha Brilliance. Before doing so for full twelve hundred years, he partook of all the fragrant flowers, oils, resins, and incense, and also anointed himself with sweet un-guents. Finally, he bathed in perfumed oil, wrapped himself in a celestial garment and, by his transcendent will, burnt his body as a sweet-smelling offering to the Buddha who had revealed to him The Lotus. Its brightness illumined worlds numerous as the sands of millions of Ganges rivers. It is in this chapter that we first meet with dharanis, or magic spells. When the Buddha Brilliance enters Nirvana, it is to his disciple Beautiful that he commits The Lotus Law, bidding him distribute his relics and erect over them thousands of stupas. After burning the Buddha's body, the disciple collected 84,000 relics and over each built an immense and beautiful stupa. Still not satisfied, he burnt off his arms in homage, but after a vast interval, during which he was honoured of gods, men, and demons, his arms were restored to him. Therefore, if any one "is able to burn a finger of his hand, or even a toe of his foot, in homage to a Buddha's stupa, he will surpass him who pays homage with domains, cities, wives, children" and so on. It was this disciple Beautiful who became the King of Healing, and such is said to be the power of this his sutra, that "if a man be sick, on hearing it his sickness will instantly disappear, and he will neither grow old nor die".

The next Chapter XXIV tells the story of the Bodhisattva Wonder-Sound, in the realm of the Buddha, King Wisdom of the Pure-flower Constellation. He had attained to a great number of samadhis, or trance-like concentrations, the names of which are given. Seeing the ray of light from Śakyamuni Buddha's brow, he seeks permission to visit this world. The Buddha-king warns him that this is a world of great ruggedness, "full of earth, stones, hills, and filth, the body of the Buddha is short and small, and all his Bodhisattvas are small of stature". Then Wonder-Sound enters into a samadhi, and first projects 84,000 jewel lotus-flowers, with stalks of gold, on to Mount Gridhrakuta, a sign which Śakyamuni recognizes as portending a visit from Wonder-Sound with his 84,000 disciples. Manjuśri asks the reason, whereupon the Ancient Buddha, Infinite Treasures, (who departed in Chapter XXII) is reintroduced calling on Wonder-Sound to reveal himself. Then is told the story of his previous existences, how he had lived as a god or a demon, a king or a citizen, a monk or a woman. He is able to transform himself at will in order to save the living through The Lotus doctrine.

The importance of Chapter XXV lies chiefly in its being the oldest reference we have to the Bodhisattva Avalokiteśvara, translated into Chinese as Kwan-yin, into Japanese as Kwannon, and commonly known among Occidentals as The Goddess of Mercy. Being asked by the Bodhisattva, Infinite Thought, why this Bodhisattva is known as Kwan-si-yin, "Regarder of the Cries of the World", the Buddha replies, it is because whoever in pain and distress call upon Kwan-yin their cries will instantly be heard and answered. If they fall into fire it will not burn them, nor floods drown, nor gales destroy. The cry of one will save all the company. The menacing sword will be snapped, and the wicked demon be unable to see the suppliant; the prisoner, guilty or innocent, will be released; the jewel-trader in peril on the road will be protected; the sufferer from carnal passion, anger, infatuation or other moral difficulties will be freed from them; women desiring sons will bear them, happy, virtuous, and wise; or, if daughters, then good in looks and character, beloved by all. Whoever worships myriads of other Bodhisattvas has vast merit, but whoever only worships Kwan-yin equals the other in merit. Kwan-yin appears in infinite forms according to the need of those to be saved, and those forms are described without reserve.

Dharanis, or Spells, are the subject of Chapter XXVI. They are described as spells for the protection of preachers of The Lotus. The first are put into the mouth of the King of Healing, and the Buddha extols them. Some are spoken of as spells used by Buddhas numerous as the sands of sixty-two kotis of Ganges. Other spells are offered, even the demons bringing their contribution to protect the Preacher of The Lotus.

The story of King Resplendent is the burden of Chapter XXVII. He dwelt in the realm of the Buddha Thunder Voice. His wife named Pure Virtue had two sons, Pure Treasury and Pure Eyed. He himself at first was a heretic, though his wife and sons were devout Buddhists. The sons were earnestly desirous of going to hear The Lotus preached, but the mother urged them first to obtain their father's permission. To convince him of their powers and fitness for the undertaking, they performed supernatural deeds, springing high into the sky, walking, sitting, lying there; the lower part of their bodies emitting fire, the upper water, or vice versa; vanishing, appearing, walking on water and so on. Convinced at last, the father decides to accompany them to hear the Buddha Thunder Voice, whereupon all the 84,000 ladies of the King's court hail The Lotus truth. King Resplendent at once makes over his domain to his younger brother, while he, his queen, his two sons and all their retinue forsake home and follow the Way of the Buddha. The two sons who have done this Buddha-deed of converting their father are richly rewarded, one becomes the King of Healing, the other the Lord of Healing.

The final Chapter XXVIII is devoted to Encouragement of the Bodhisattva Universal Virtue. He had come from the eastern quarter with all his vast train of countless gods, dragons, yakshas, and all the beings of his realm, to hear The Lotus preached. On his arrival he vows to guard all who believe this Sutra, so that wherever any such a one walks or stands, reading or reciting this Sutra, he will at once mount his royal six-tusked elephant and with a host of great Bodhisattvas go to that place and, revealing himself, will protect him and comfort his mind; moreover, if any one forgets a single word or verse he will put it again into his memory. He will also give him dharanis, or magic spells, to ward off all foes, and to these spells he now gives utterance. All such disciples of The Lotus will ever do the works of Universal Virtue and their heads will be caressed by the Tathagatas. If any recite or copy the Sutra they will avoid every evil destiny and go straight to Maitreya's heaven. To him the Buddha replies in similar terms, adding that any one who recites or copies this Sutra, is in reality attending on the Buddha; moreover is as if hearing him speak it with his lips, and as if covered with his robe. Such a one will later sit on a lion throne amid a great assembly of gods and men. By the power of this Sutra such disciples will no longer be attached to clothes, bed-covers, drink, food, or other transient things. If any one contemn them he will be blind for generation on generation, if he tells their faults, true or false, he will be smitten with leprosy; if he ridicules them, his teeth for

33

generations will be sparse and missing, his lips vile, his nose flat, his hands and feet contorted, his eyes asquint, his body stinking and filthy with evil scabs and bloody pus, he will be dropsical and short of breath and have every evil disease. But those that bless and reverence him who reads or recites the Sutra will receive abundant rewards here and now.

Doctrine

Reverence for the Bible in the West has its counterpart among Far Eastern Buddhists in the reverence shown to the Sutras, especially to The Lotus. There is, perhaps, less restraint there in the expression of devotion. Such reverence is a natural consequence of the belief that The Lotus is the Ultimate Truth preached by every Buddha, once only in every Buddha-world, past, present, and to come. To the Mahayanist it is therefore the Eternal Gospel of Buddhism in all worlds and through all time. The Sutra is declared to be the last will and testament of Sakyamuni before his departure; it is his final bequest to this world. All his previous teaching is postulated as interim doctrine, that is, during the time of the disciples' ignorance and while their minds were still bound by earth-ties and myopic vision. This final revelation is said to have been reserved by him until the eve of his Nirvana. In it he at last makes known the All-Truth, which confers Perfect Enlightenment and Final Nirvana, or Liberation. This supreme liberation cannot be attained by self-discipline and works; it can only be attained by faith

34

and invocation. Salvation by Faith is then the fundamental doctrine of the Mahayana School. According to The Lotus teaching no sacrifice is required, no expiation, no atonement, no remorse, no repentance in the sense of contrition, nothing but faith in the infinite mercy and infinite power of the Infinite Buddha who lives and reigns for ever.

It is manifest, then, that the spiritual message of the book is revolutionary in its character. Not only are these doctrines of salvation given, but there is presented the panorama of unlimited universes, all of them ever-changing manifestations of the All-Buddha, of whom Śakyamuni is but one expression in one of infinite worlds; the assurance that the Eternal Buddha is both transcendent and immanent; the teaching that every world, every universe, is a flower of the Eternal Lotus; the call to faith as a greater force than disciplinary or ascetic works; the proclamation of the Eternal Buddha, and of his Salvation for all, even to the devils in hell; the assurance of the ultimate enlightenment of all; the universality of buddhahood for all, because all are potential buddhas, or enlightened ones—such is the inspiration of this masterpiece of literature.

The author is clearly conscious that he is boldly putting into the Buddha's lips doctrines to which he never gave utterance, and which are not found in the orthodox scriptures. So eager is he to explain, or explain away, this fundamental discrepancy, that he devotes several chapters and parables to elucidation of and excuse for the Buddha's complete reversal of his

35

earlier teaching. At times he openly fears that the Buddha will be accused of having deceived his disciples and even lied to them. Unbiased minds, as well as the biased minds of the orthodox, cannot fail to recognize that the orthodox doctrines and those of The Lotus are diametrically opposed. There is, therefore, good reason why the author, who so skillfully foists the new doctrine on to Śakyamuni, should endeavour to defend his position by pretending that all the Buddha's life had been spent in teaching an interim doctrine, using the methods of a tactician or a casuist. The author is indeed in serious difficulty. He wishes to father on to Śakyamuni, the founder of Buddhism, doctrines he would have repudiated, and to use Śakyamuni's name and authority to change entirely the character of his religion. If this view be correct, then the pious fraud has been remarkably successful, for it is this form of Buddhism that has tamed savage tribes such as the Mongols and Tibetans, inspired people like the Chinese and Japanese to a higher spiritual and artistic development, established a cult with many resemblances to Christianity, and is now reacting, chiefly through theosophical publications, on certain lines of thought in the West. Orthodox Buddhism has had no such influence. It is the heterodox school that has prevailed.

Needless to say, the above explanation is not acceptable to the devout Mahayanist. Like the Fundamentalist in the West he refuses to have his faith shaken in the letter of the Law. The Lotus, in his estimate, was spoken by Sakyamuni on earth during his last years, all his previous teaching having been preparatory. Many disciples, who are represented as unable to receive his ultimate Truth, left him as is shown in Chapter II, where they turn away from the higher revelation.

Bound to the letter of his scripture, the devout Mahayanist refuses to see in this dramatic work a brilliant apocalypse, in which the earthly Buddha and his disciples are used as figures to portray a new religion of Salvation for all. That in reality is the term which indicates the character of the new and revolutionary doctrine. It accounts also for the division between Mahayanist and Hinayanist, the broad and the narrow schools, the believer in universal salvation by faith and the believer in the salvation of the few by works. It is self-evident that these two terms are not the creation of the orthodox, for they would never dub themselves Hinayanists, men of the "small cart". That term is a Mahayanist creation, and the influence of The Lotus Sutra in fixing the contrasted terms is undoubted.

The author of The Lotus drama puts into the mouth of Sakyamuni the statement:

"In the Buddha-lands of the Universe
There is only the One-Vehicle Law, (Mahayana)
Neither a second, nor a third."

The other ways, or wains, he says are only "provisional terms", meant

"To lead all living beings
Toward the true Buddha-wisdom";

because a Buddha

> "Never by a small vehicle (Hinayana)
> Really saves the living;"

for, being in the Great Vehicle (Mahayana) himself,
he says:

> "If by a small vehicle
> I converted but one human being,
> I should thereby fall into selfishness,
> A thing that cannot be."

Having vowed to lead all beings into perfect buddhahood along with himself, he must do so by the highest
means, by the fullest enlightenment, by buddhahood;
it was only as a temporary expedient that he had led
his disciples by partial truths on the way to the All-
Truth. This idea is especially brought out in the
parables of The Burning House, Chapter III, and
the Magic City, Chapter VII.

Leaving then "this pious fraud", as the Orthodox
believe, to implicate itself by its own excuses, let us
turn to certain other doctrines of the book, which
differentiate it from the orthodox school.

I. Buddhism, whose awakening is placed under the
shelter of the bo or bodhi-tree (*ficus religiosa*), the
Buddhist tree of knowledge, bases its existence on
gnosis. Mental awakening, or awareness, intelligence,
mind, knowledge, wisdom, are all implicit within the
term. To what extent the Gnostics were indebted to
Buddhism is not yet clearly elucidated. Mind to both
was the supreme factor. But though mind was funda-

mental to his doctrine, Śakyamuni, according to the Orthodox school, recognized no Mind behind mind. Like Socrates he treated, and was justified in treating, the theistic conceptions of his day as of inferior value. He did not deny the existence of the gods, but placed them beneath the position attained by a Buddha, that is a truly enlightened man. This Mindless system is entirely changed in Mahayanism, in which the Eternal Buddha, who may be described as the Eternal Mind and Eternal Soul, becomes the very foundation of the new structure.

In The Lotus, when the Ancient Buddha appears, who resembles "The Ancient of Days", it is evident that He is a Person and the devout see in him the Mind behind the All. The Lotus itself, in its complete aspect, is considered as but a metaphor for the Universe, each flower a world; it is used also for the nidus of a soul, as from the spiritual Lotus-flower springs a soul or a life. That the Mahayanists believe in the Mind behind The Lotus, or the All, is clear from the emphasis they lay on the Eternal Buddha. He is in and through all things, which in a sense is the Buddhist form of Pantheism, although, in fact, transcendence rather than immanence is the doctrine of our Sutra. It is manifest, for instance, that the Ancient Buddha is transcendent; when he appears all beings are shown to be his rather than in him; all must assemble to hear Śakyamuni, his earthly counterpart, proclaim The Lotus, with its gospel of universal salvation. It may be argued that the Ancient Buddha here revealed was only one form of the

Eternal Buddha, but, even so, the accepted interpretation is that he is the Eternal Buddha. At any rate Nirvana, as extinction of existence, is demonstrated by Mahayanists to be a false doctrine of the Hinayana School.

Chapter XVI is considered to be the supreme declaration of the Buddha, in its Revelation of the eternity of his life. It is Sakyamuni, the earthly form of Buddha, who speaks. After telling of his earthly enlightenment, he goes on to say that though his hearers, who have been his disciples during his brief earthly career, may think such enlightenment a comparatively recent event, yet in reality since he veritably became Buddha, infinite, boundless, hundreds, thousands, myriads, kotis, nayutas, of kalpas, or aeons, had passed. In other words, he who on earth was Sakyamuni had already been Buddha, the Enlightened One, through infinite ages. The doctrine bears resemblance to the doctrine of Eternal Sonship in certain forms of Christian theology. This idea of the infinite is shown in meticulous terms, which to the Western mind may seem puerile. The word "infinite" might cover all our needs. But the story-teller knew his hearers. A single word would pass meaninglessly over their minds. To an unlettered audience his method of detailed illustration had greater value.

The Buddha, then, is conceived of in terms of Omniscience and Eternity. His omnipotence also is shown, by his power to call all creatures to his assembly and to shake all creation. While transcendent, he is also in a sense omnipresent, in that he can send his searchlight ray into every world, and can appear anywhere at will. Little stress is laid in this Sutra on his creative and destroying power. This may be taken as assumed, for every Buddha-world springs as a flower, flourishes and perishes, only to be resurrected in some other form. In this sense the Eternal Buddha is creator, destroyer, and eternal re-creator of worlds.

Perhaps the most interesting reference to the character of the Tathagata, or Buddha, in his power of spiritual omnipresence, is seen in the beautiful saying in Chapter X, "The Dwelling of the Tathagata is the great compassionate heart within all living beings; the Robe of the Tathagata is the gentle and forbearing heart; the Throne of the Tathagata is the spirituality of all existence". Again: "Though I am in another domain, yet will I reveal myself from time to time to the preacher of The Lotus. If he forgets any detail of this Sutra I will return and tell him, so that he may perfectly possess it."

II. Not only is there an Eternal Mind behind the All, but Mahayanism goes further. It places this Eternal Mind, or Eternal Buddha, in the relationship of Father. The Lotus in Chapter II says that the Buddha is "the Father of all worlds, who forever brings to an end all fear, despondency, distress, ignorance, and enveloping gloom, and brings to perfection boundless knowledge, strength, and courage. He is born in the world to save all living creatures from the fires of birth, age, disease, death, grief, suffering, infatuation, darkness, and the three

poisons, and teach them to obtain perfect enlightenment".

III. The Eternal Buddha limits his omnipotence
by the freewill of his offspring. He may not, for
instance, use force to save them. In the parable of
the Burning House, in Chapter III, though the lord
of the house is strong in body and limb he may not
carry out his children. They must come out of their
own will. This is shown again in Chapter IV, in the
parable of the Prodigal Son, who leaves his father,
and runs away. For long he wanders and the father
seeks him in vain. After a vain search, the father
settles in a certain city, builds a palatial home, amasses
great wealth, and is surrounded by innumerable
servants and every luxury; but still he is sore at heart,
mourning his lost son. The son meanwhile wanders
from town to village and village to town, all his money
gone, clad in rags, and hiring out his services for a
wretched meal. At last, one day, his travels lead him
to his father's mansion and grounds, where he sees
his unrecognized father surrounded with honour and
glory. Fearing lest he be seized as a slave he turns
hastily away, but not before his father has seen and
known him. Then comes the account of the son's
arrest, his terror, his liberation, his being persuaded
to undertake work, the most menial work, his gradual
rise to be major-domo, and the climax when he is
declared as son and heir.

One feature clearly evident in this parable is that
the freewill of the son is recognized, persuasion being
the only method the father might use.

IV. In the above parable the relationship of sonship is clearly shown. To summarize the long and detailed reply of the disciples, the rich lord is the Buddha and we are all the Buddha's sons. The Buddha has always declared us as his sons. We, too, have wandered away and gone through all the miseries of life, being attached to lower things, but now the Buddha-wisdom is revealed to us, and we know that we are Buddha-sons. No longer must we hanker after the smaller vehicles, the hinayana, for now we are in the Great Vehicle, the mahayana; no longer are we, so to speak, struggling children of earth, but sons of the Omniscient. The Great Treasure of the King of Truth unsought has come to us, and we have obtained all the inheritance of Buddha-sons.

V. Again, the love of the Buddha to all creatures is equal and universal. This finds expression in various places, as, for instance, in the Parable of the Trees and Grasses in Chapter V. On these the Buddha-rain falls impartially, as does his saving truth on all creatures. His truth and his salvation are equally for all beings universally.

VI. Karma and Anatman are fundamental doctrines of original Buddhism. To the Buddha there was no such entity as the atman, which may be expressed as the eternal, individual soul. Personality during life was recognized. It was, however, only a bundle of sensations; at death when these sensations ceased for lack of organs, the bundle or person ceased to exist as such. But there remained karma, or the deeds done, which may in a sense be described as character without a rigid personality; this remainder entered into a new bundle linked, even consciously, with the past.

"The Karma—all that total of a soul
Which in the things it did, the thought it had,
The self it wove—with woof of viewless time."

The Light of Asia.

Therefore, it might be said that the sinner suffered, while the saint rose to the condition of nirvana, or extinction, though whether annihilation of existence or merely cessation of reincarnation was meant is disputed. In Mahayanism, however, the atman or immortal soul is restored, and is no longer karma or character without continued personality, merely the progressive resultant of all previous deeds in infinite past existences. While cause and effect remain in the ethical realm, factors of saving power and even of something resembling works of supererogation are introduced. These are not opposed to the law of causation but fulfil it vicariously, or by a process of substitution. Moral good and evil remain essential to life, but they can be attained without struggle and effort by the process of faith. Faith can thus change the entire aspect and force of karma. Instantaneous conversion of the whole nature is assured by faith and invocation, through the medium of a new relationship. Old infrangible determinist bonds snap like tow under the liberating influence of a new personal relationship with a personal, all-loving Buddha-Father. The likeness to the doctrines of the Fatherhood of God and Salvation by faith of the Four

Gospels and the Johannine Epistles is even more remarkable than is the Buddhist ritual to the Roman rite, that "invention of the devil to embarrass Mother Church". The fundamental truth in the Mahayanist texts, as in Christian dogma, has been of course decked out with trappings ill suited to its original simplicity.

VII. The Bodhisattvas, throughout The Lotus, are shown as Enlighteners and Saviours. That is their office and, in consequence, every true disciple becomes a bodhisattva, a being of enlightenment. A distinction is made between Great Bodhisattvas in the spirit world, and ordinary bodhisattvas in this and other similar worlds. The past transmigrations of certain of the more prominent Bodhisattva-disciples, as well as their future, are told; but, in the main body of the narrative, we are spared the more extravagant and even repulsive stories of self-sacrifice by Buddhas and Bodhisattvas. Something of it occurs in the apocryphal chapters about the imaginary Bodhisattvas, such as the Lord of Healing and Kwan-yin. The fact of their mention in Kumarajiva's Chinese version is evidence of the existence of their cult early in our era. The Bodhisattvas are qualified to enter the bliss of the Buddhas, but delay for themselves this privilege by the vow they make to save every living being in the Buddha-realm in which they dwell. The one who is most famous in the Far East is Amitabha, of Eternal Light and Eternal Life, possibly a conception derived from Western Asia; his name does not appear in The Lotus. Maitreya, a name suggestive of a Mithraic origin, is foretold in

45

The Lotus as the next earthly Buddha. It may be mentioned here that every earthly Buddha-period is of limited duration. It is said to last through three stages, that of the true law, that of semblance of the true law (or formalism, the form without the power), and that of final decadence and disappearance, after which a new Buddha with a new Buddha-period appears. Maitreya, or in Chinese Mi-le Fo, is the Bodhisattva who is to appear as the Buddha of the new period, and he is constantly invoked now as the Coming Buddha, the Messiah who will restore all things.

VIII. Salvation by Faith or Invocation. According to the teaching of The Lotus, while the earthly Buddha did, until near his end, teach the law of salvation by works, it was only because his disciples were earth-bound and their spiritual eyes were not yet opened, nor as yet could be opened. The author knows well that he is introducing a revolution in Buddhism. He sees clearly that the new doctrine of salvation by Faith as the ultimate, indeed the only way, or vehicle, is a very different method from that which in India was accepted as the doctrine of Sakya-muni. The clearest evidence that can be offered of this fact, indubitable to all but the interested, lies in the repudiation of the new doctrine by the Orthodox school, as a contradiction of the essential teaching of the Founder. The "Northern" School may dub it Hinayana, if they wish; it prefers to stand by the documents, and to be fundamentalist with its Master, Sakyamuni, than universalist dependent on

46

pious fiction. The author himself realizes that he is confronted with serious difficulty in defending his apocalyptic Buddha from the charge of deception and lying, terms he himself uses. He labours hard with statement and parable to show that the Buddha had not been guilty of falsehood, but had given his disciples such glimpses of truth as they were temporarily able to realize, until they could bear the full light. Consequently, he declares salvation by works to have been but a tactical and temporary teaching, in preparation for the revelation of the doctrine of universal salvation by faith, especially by faith in The Lotus Sutra. The Mahayanist admits all the Hinayana texts and honours them, though they are to him but an interim ethic; in addition he has his own vast treasury of sutras and other works. It is the teaching of these, of which this Sutra is to most the chief, that revelation is made of the All-truth which brings liberation, liberation not by works of the law, but by faith. Salvation by faith is then the foundation doctrine of the Mahayana School. This doctrine easily degenerated into Salvation by invocation through the teaching of the Sutra itself. Such teaching is seen in Chapter X. It produced a degeneration which reduced Buddhist prayer, or rather invocation, to machine-like repetition. It is often literally machine-made, as witness the prayer-wheels or rotatory prayer-drums, large and small, stationary or portable, of the Lamaistic sect. Indeed, invocation flags float in every breeze in the fields of China in protection of the crops. The rosary —is it parent or child of the Western rosary?—is

47

carried by monks and nuns and by the devout, and Namo Amitabha is repeated millions of times daily. The Buddhist rosary is perhaps as useful a mode of emptying the mind and reaching the "void" as any other, if we may judge by results. Here is a quotation from Chapter X of The Lotus on the value of invocation and especially of the repetition of the Sutra:

"The Buddha addressed the Lord of Healing saying: . . . if there be any who hears but a single verse, or a single word of the Wonderful Law-flower Sutra, and by a single thought delights in it, I also predict for him complete and perfect enlightenment. And let there be any who receive and keep, read and recite, or expound and copy even a single verse in the Lotus Sutra, or devoutly look upon the Sutra with reverence as if it were the Buddha, or make offerings to it in various ways with flowers, perfumes, garlands, sandal-powder, perfumed unguents, incense for burning, silk-canopies, banners, flags, garments, music, or even revere it with folded hands; know, Lord of Healing, (this is evidence that) such people have already (in past transmigrations) paid homage to ten myriad kotis of Buddhas and under those Buddhas performed their vows. (Hence they are born among men and) these are the people who will certainly be first to become Buddhas in future worlds. These are the people to be honoured even now, for they have recognized the infinite value of The Lotus Sutra. If such people should be able even by stealth to preach to one person but one word of the Sutra, they reveal thereby that they are Tathagata messengers sent by the Tathagata to perform Tathagata deeds. Any one who sins other grievous sins, even blasphemy against the Buddha, is only a light sinner compared with him who with a single ill word defames the devotee of this Sutra (for that is the sin so to speak against the Holy Ghost). The preacher of the Lotus should be honoured above all men and gifts showered upon him, for the Lotus is the Treasury of the mystic secret of all Buddhas, guarded by all Buddhas and seldom divulged. Wherever it is preached, there a stupa of precious materials should be erected, which should be served with all kinds of flowers &c., &c., music and hymns."

The supreme value of The Lotus is shown in Chapter XIV, in the parable of the King who, to reward his brave soldiers, shares with them everything he possesses, only reserving to himself the superb jewel on his brow. At last, seeing the splendid deeds of his soldiers, he decides to give them also even this supreme gift. So is it with the Tathagata; seeing his followers fight so bravely against the hosts of Mara, he at length gives them the greatest reward of all—the entry into Salvation by faith and sonship in the priceless Jewel of his forehead, The Lotus Sutra, the Sutra which can only be preached once in a Buddha realm. The obtaining of this jewel will bring infinite enlightenment, ultimate wisdom, the full and complete Way of the Buddha.

IX. It has already been shown that a permanent personal soul has taken the place of the Buddha's

49

anatman, or no-soul. The bundle of sensations is no longer a temporary organism dissolved at death, but an entity personal and lasting. To the school which postulates Nirvana as the final extinction of existence, the Mahayanist opposes the doctrine of eternal life. Transmigration and the hells remain, for, as seen in Chapters I and VII, the projection of the Buddha-ray reveals the hells of every world with their suffering creatures; nowhere are the appalling sufferings in hell portrayed more realistically than in Mahayanist temples. A universalist doctrine logically requires that the hells of every world shall come to an end in the ultimate salvation of all its creatures, especially when they hear and respond to the proclamation of The Lotus gospel. The hells and transmigrations through all grades of existence, whether gods, devils, men, or creatures of every species, are still necessary in every world, though all may escape on responding to the good news of The Lotus. Their escape is not to extinction, but to the glories of other Buddha-realms, which in this Sutra are shown to be infinite in variety, number, and splendour. While all will attain to perfect enlightenment and happiness it is given to some to progress to even higher offices. During infinite time in infinite worlds there are infinite Buddhas and Buddha-realms. The most exalted positions therefore are open to those who have the spiritual capacity for them. Take, for instance, the prediction in Chapter VI of the future of the disciple Maha-Kaśyapa. It is foretold that he will pay homage (as disciple) to three hundred myriad kotis of universally-honoured Buddhas, serving, revering, honouring, extolling them, and widely proclaiming the infinite Truth of those Buddhas. Presumably he is a disciple of each Buddha separately one after another, thus continuing through incalculable aeons. In his final transmigration it is prophesied that he also will become a Buddha in human form, whose name will be Radiance Tathagata, worshipful, all-wise, of perfectly enlightened conduct, well-departed, understander of the world, peerless leader, controller, teacher of gods and men, Buddha, world-honoured one, whose domain is named Radiant Virtue, and whose Buddha-kalpa, or epoch, is named Magnificence. His lifetime as Buddha will be for twelve kalpas. His law in its correctness will abide (after him) for twenty kalpas and the Semblance of his law, before it begins its final decay, will also abide for twenty kalpas. The period given to Maha-Kaśyapa, as happy disciple of incalculable numbers of Buddhas and himself as a Buddha, is certainly beyond human conception, but whether he then goes into the retirement of some final Nirvana, endlessly radiant and happy, is not foretold. This, however, seems to be the meaning of the author's Buddha (Śakyamuni) when he speaks of his own immediate Nirvana, which evidently does not mean non-existence, but a state of super-existence, such as that of the Ancient Buddha of Chapter XI. At any rate, it may be said that the Buddha-domain of Kaśyapa, as of the other disciples, while described in all the glories of an oriental paradise, is never depicted in terms of sensuality.

We may say, then, that the soul continues its personal life, if not endlessly, yet in duration beyond the calculation of mundane arithmetic, that the hells and suffering are impermanent; that bliss is ultimately universal in every Buddha-realm; that infinite possibilities in infinite realms and infinite time are open to all; and that for the highest, that is, those who attain to ultimate perfect enlightenment, there is a supreme Nirvana, ineffable, beyond human definition or conception.

X. The clerical order has due encouragement in the Sutra. Monks and nuns of all types, good, bad, and indifferent, receive mention. The type commanding praise is the devoted preacher of The Lotus doctrine, and him the Buddhas and Bodhisattvas will always defend, support, and inspire. In Chapter XIV the character of such a one is depicted and in Chapter XX special attention is drawn to a certain long-suffering monk called "Never-despise", because he saw in every creature a prospective buddha and revered it accordingly, to the annoyance of his fellow monks, at whose hands he suffered much ill-treatment, until at length he himself became Buddha.

In conclusion, it is just to say that, although The Lotus Sutra is undoubtedly a fundamental classic in Mahayanism, as well as the most popular, the number of its readers is small in relation to the population. This is especially the case in China, where it is known to relatively few; at least 95 per cent. of Chinese adults are quite unable to read it, as is probably also the fact among the monks themselves. The same remark would probably apply to Tibet and Mongolia. In Japan both people and monks are better educated, and therefore must be classed in a different category. In consequence, the number of monks and people in China possessed of any working acquaintance with the Sutra is very small. Moreover, simple though the language is, much of it is still beyond the apprehension of the ordinary reader, partly because of the numerous Sanskrit terms, partly because of the special meaning read into ordinary Chinese terms, and partly because the book needs an interpreter with insight. Apocalyptic literature is necessarily mystical, even paradoxical and occult. The literalist will either be repelled or attracted by the mystery. His vision is held by minor detail. He is devoid of capacity for seeing with the eyes of the apocalyptic author, the religious dramatist. For this reason the devotee of The Lotus Sutra in the East, like the literalist interpreter of The Bible in the West, rarely gets within sight of the stage and the play. The individual actor and his individual movements, even his individual words rivet the attention, and the drama is lost in its detail.

Here, then, is one of the great religious dramas of the world. The composer knows that he is offering a new Buddhism in place of the religion of the Founder. He conceives that Founder as declaring a new Gospel, but places him on the stage of the Vulture Peak, where in India he had often addressed his disciples. There he discloses, by means of the all-revealing Buddha-ray, the concept of infinite worlds in infinite space and time, with vast numbers of Buddhas teaching their infinite numbers of disciples. Yet these Buddhas later are revealed as the offspring of the one eternal Buddha. The scene changes and, awakening from a trance, the Buddha of, or in, this world announces his intention to reveal a truth that will shake the universe and also turn from him many of his disciples. Then, hesitatingly and with reluctance, he makes the great revelation that Buddhahood, like to his own, is of immediate attainment and within the ready reach of all. We see a host of disciples, the Hinayanists, shocked by this *volte-face*, withdraw from the august assembly, because the Buddha has shattered all the doctrine he has taught them in the past, and is no longer to be trusted. Then we see the Buddha explaining, even excusing himself, to the faithful who remain. After this he predicts the future of his disciples, and prepares them for the great truths they are to retell, in the parables of the Burning House, the Seeking Father, or Prodigal Son, the Rain, the Magic City, and others. The supreme scene opens with the appearance of the great jewelled shrine in the sky, from which comes the voice of the Buddha of old. The stage is then filled by the arrival of Buddhas, with their train, from every part of the universe. And, at last, the Buddha of old is revealed to the assembled host in dramatic fashion, by the ascent into the sky of Śakyamuni Buddha. The great drama proceeds in the raising of the whole assembly of his disciples from the mountain peak into the air, to join the celestial durbar. Still others arrive from other universes, and the sky is thronged with a glorious company from all worlds and in all stages of existence. Marvels appear, miracles are performed, Bodhisattvas as the sands of innumerable Ganges come to make manifest the incalculable number of Sakyamuni's disciples. The climax of the drama is reached when Sakyamuni makes the declaration that in reality he, too, is the Eternal Buddha. After a certain interlude, he dismisses the assembly who are seen withdrawing from the celestial stage, and finally the shrine of the Ancient of Days disappears from the sky.

The doctrine taught, whatever its origin, is as revolutionary to Buddhism as was the doctrine of Our Lord to Judaism. In the Gospels we have a human figure treading the human stage of action, commanding the affection of the common people, disturbing the vested interests of ceremonialists and legists, ending in a cruel death, and a further revelation to certain disciples. In the Hinayana texts we have a human teacher who, having diagnosed the cause of the disease of transmigration, teaches his disciples an ethical remedy by mental control and discipline. In Mahayana, especially as portrayed in The Lotus Sutra, we have a dramatic presentation, reminding us of the Revelation of St. John at Patmos, with his vision of "One like unto the Son of Man" who was yet "Alpha and Omega", "the first and the last", together with the angels and the heavenly host, the sealed book, the vials, and so on. In this great Sutra we have a dramatic presentation of a glorified earthly

55

Buddha, who is yet a Buddha from of old, an eternal Buddha, together with an incalculable host of Buddhas and of all intelligent beings in the universe, assembled at a vast meeting in the sky, when the revelation of the last and ultimate Lotus doctrine is made. The whole is the creation of a brilliant dramatist whose name is unknown, but who has left behind if not the greatest, then one of the greatest religious dramas in the world.

THE LOTUS SUTRA

3. Maya's conception of her son, the Buddha, who arrives for reincarnation on a white elephant

I

"ONCE the Buddha (Śakyamuni) was staying at the City of Royal Palaces (Rajagriha), and on the Vulture Peak (Gridhrakuta) assembled a great host of his greater monks, in all twelve thousand . . . emancipated from every bond and free in mind."

There follows a list of names of his well-known disciples, together with the names of his foster-mother and the mother of his son, with their train of disciples. Assembled also were eighty thousand Great Bodhisattvas who had attained to perfect enlightenment. A number of their names are given, including Manjuśri, Kwan-yin, the Lord of Healing and Maitreya. There were present also twenty thousand of the gods, including Brahma; also Dragon-kings, Kinnara-kings, Gandharva-kings, Asura-kings, Garuda-kings, all kings of the lower worlds and lower orders of being, each with hundreds of thousands of followers. The disciples, and the others, who might almost be described as angels, archangels, and all the hosts of the heavens and the hells, fall down in worship at the Buddha's feet.

"At that time the World-honoured One, surrounded, worshipped, revered, honoured and extolled by the four groups of disciples, preached for all bodhisattvas, the Mahayana sutra called 'The Meaning of Infinity'."

Immediately afterwards he entered into the trance, or contemplation, described as "The Station of the Meaning of Infinity", the heavens raining down on him divine flowers and the whole universe being shaken.

While the vast assembly looked on the Buddha in amaze, he

"sent forth from the curl of white hair between his eyebrows a ray of light, which illuminated eighteen thousand worlds in the eastern quarter, so that there was nowhere it did not reach, downwards to the lowest hell and upward to the highest heaven of each world. Here, in this our own world, were then made visible in those vast domains their living beings in the six states of existence; likewise were seen the Buddhas at present existing in those lands. The doctrines those Buddhas were preaching could be clearly heard; and in those worlds were revealed the monks, nuns and disciples of both sexes",

also their Bodhisattvas, their Buddhas who had attained Nirvana, and the Stupas for the relics of those Buddhas erected after their respective departures.

Maitreya is now presented inquiring of Manjuśri the meaning of this wonderful manifestation, while he describes to him, first in prose then in verse, the marvels they are beholding:

"The ray from between his brows
Illumines the eastern quarter
Of the eighteen thousand worlds,
Colouring them all with gold.

From their Avici-hells
To the Summit of All-Existence,
The living in those worlds,
The destinies of unborn and dying,
I behold them all from here.
In those distant lands I see
Bodhisattvas like sands of Ganges,
Who in every varying degree
Seek the Buddha-Way.
Some there are who give alms,
Gold, silver and coral,
Pearls and felicitous gems,
Moonstones and cornelian,
Diamonds and precious things,
Male and female slaves,
Fine carriages and horses,
Jewelled palanquins and litters,
These alms they give with joy,
Turning to the Buddha-way,
Seeking to gain this Vehicle,
The supreme in the Triple World.

   •   •   •   •   •

Also I see bodhisattvas
Give their flesh, hands and feet,
And their wives and children, as alms,
To find the Supreme Way.
Again I see bodhisattvas
Giving their heads, eyes, bodies,
Cheerfully as alms,
To find the Buddha-wisdom."

He sees also kings leaving their palaces, shaving their heads, and putting on the monk's robe to seek the Buddha-way. He sees bodhisattvas who

> "Enter the depths of the mountains
> To ponder the Buddha-way."

And

> "Dwellers in secluded wilds
> In profoundest concentration
> To obtain transcendent powers."

Others

> "Profoundly wise and resolute,
> Are able to question the Buddhas
> And apprehend all they hear.

. . . . .

> I see, too, Buddha-sons
> Expounding the Truth to the multitude,
> Cheerfully preaching the Law,
> Converting bodhisattvas
> And, having defeated the army of Mara,
> Beating the drum of the Law."

He sees other bodhisattvas, who

> "Dwelling in forests, emjt radiance
> That saves the sufferers in hell,
> Leading them into the Buddha-way."

He sees also Buddha-sons who,

> "Abiding in the strength of long-suffering,
> Though men of utmost arrogance
> Hate, abuse and beat them,
> Are able through all to endure,
> To find the Puddha-way."

Others are seen bestowing dainties, drink and food, medicines, and robes of priceless value, precious buildings of sandal-wood, flowers, fruits, and bathing-pools on the Buddhas while seeking the Supreme Way. Buddha-sons are seen building numberless stupas, adorned with precious jewels, bells, and streamers, in homage to the Buddhas, the light from such stupas illuminating their lands.

Though the Buddha has emitted but one solitary ray, and only in one of the six directions of space, yet all these worlds are revealed. Why, asks Maitreya, has he shed so wondrous a light? Is it that he is now about to reveal some mystic truth? The host of gods, men, and spirits of the underworld yearn for an answer.

Manjuśri replies that he believes the Buddha is now about to make his final revelation, "to preach the Great Law, to pour the rain of the Great Law, to blow the conch of the Great Law, to beat the drum of the Great Law, to expound the meaning of the Great Law". He says that whenever in the past such a Buddha-ray has been emitted it has always preceded the declaration of the Wonderful Law to all creatures. He says he has seen this before, under a Buddha named Light-of-the-Sun-and-Moon, and under twenty thousand successive Buddhas of the same name. The last of these, before leaving home to become Buddha, had eight royal sons, whose names and story he gives; they all became Buddhas. Before the Buddha Sun-moon-light withdrew to Nirvana, he first entered into the trance-like meditation on the meaning of Infinity, whereupon flowers fell from heaven and the whole universe was shaken. On awaking from his trance he preached, through his disciple Mystic-light, "The Lotus Flower of the Wonderful Law, by which bodhisattvas are instructed", and which is under the special guardianship of the Buddhas themselves. Manjuśri thereupon reveals to the assembly that it was he himself who was Mystic-light in a previous incarnation. This is told, in both prose and verse, with a wealth of detail and in splendour of language.

THE World-honoured One, coming calmly and deliberately out of his trance, now addresses his disciple Śariputra, and through him the assembled company:

"The wisdom of Buddhas is profound and infinite. Their school of wisdom is difficult to enter and to understand." Ascetics and those who cleave to the law of works "cannot apprehend it". But a Buddha has been in fellowship with countless numbers of Buddhas, and knows all things. "Only a Buddha with a Buddha can fathom the reality of All-Existence." In verse he says:

"Of yore I followed countless Buddhas,
　And perfectly trod the Ways
　Of the profound and mystic Law,
　Hard to perceive and perform.
　During infinite kotis of kalpas,
　Having followed all these Ways,
　Attaining fruition on the Wisdom-throne
　I could perfectly understand
　The meaning of every nature and form.
　I and the Buddhas of the universe
　Alone can understand these things—
　The Truth beyond demonstration,
　The Truth beyond the realm of terms."

The wisest of his disciples, he says, will not be able to understand it, but they can apprehend it by faith. This ultimate, or absolute Truth can only be understood by Buddhas. His disciples should at once "beget great strength of faith, for at length, after his preparatory teaching, he must now proclaim the perfect Truth". His previous teaching had only been tactical and expedient, during the time of their ignorance, but now a higher Truth must be proclaimed.

Thereupon doubts arise among the strictest set of his disciples, those who by arduous effort have made the greatest progress in his previous teaching.

"For what reason", ask they one of another, "does the World honoured One now so earnestly extol this Way of expediency and utter these words: 'The Truth which the Buddha has obtained is most profound and difficult to comprehend. The meaning of what he is about to proclaim is so hard to understand that it will be beyond the grasp even of his most disciplined followers.' We have already attained to his principle of emancipation and have reached the stage of Nirvana. Now we know not whither his new principle will lead."

Śariputra voices their discontent by asking the Buddha what is his reason for extolling this method of expediency, which now is to end in the declaration of a Truth, profound and mysterious, such as they have never before heard the Buddha mention.

"O Wisdom-Sun! Great Holy Honoured One!
. . . . .

These fault-eliminated Arhats
And those who seek Nirvana
Have fallen into nets of doubt."

These workers of the Law, these disciples, gods, dragon-kings, spirits, and other beings "scan each the other in perplexity". Is all that they have learnt and done in vain?

> "The Buddha's mouth-born sons
> With folded hands expectant wait.
> Be pleased to send forth the mystic sound
> And now proclaim the Truth in reality.
> Gods, nagas, spirits and others,
> Numerous as sands of Ganges,
> Bodhisattvas aspiring to be Buddhas,
> Fully eighty thousand in number,
> Also, from myriads of kotis of lands,
> Holy Wheel-rolling Kings are here,
> With folded hands and reverent hearts
> Desiring to hear the Perfect Way."

The Buddha replies: "Enough! enough! say no more. Were I to explain this matter, the worlds of gods and men would be startled and perplexed."

Sariputra pleads:
> "King of the Law, Honoured One Most High?
> Be pleased to explain without misgiving!
> In this assembly are countless beings
> Able respectfully to believe."

Again the Buddha protests that at his preaching "all the worlds of gods, men, and demons would be startled and perplexed and the haughty among his disciples might fall into the great pit".

Once more Sariputra appeals in pleading terms, whereupon the Buddha responds to the thrice-repeated prayer. But, before he can open his mouth to speak, five thousand of his (hinayana) disciples rise from their seats, salute him, and withdraw. "The root of sin was deep in them, and their haughty spirit was so enlarged that they imagined they had already attained." The Buddha remains silent and does not stop them.

"Now, in this congregation," he says at last, "I am free from twigs and leaves, and have none but the true and real. It is good that such extremely haughty ones as these are gone away." Such is the author's dramatic way of exposing the pride of the Hinayana Buddhists in rejecting the Mahayana doctrine of universal salvation by faith, rather than by works.

Rare is the appearance of a Buddha. Like the udumbara, which is seldom seen in flower, so is it with the Buddhas. But when one appears, though he must use various expedients in his teaching, "no word of his is false". "The Buddhas seek to open (the eyes of) the living to the true Buddha-knowledge, so that they may attain to the pure (Way.") Universal attainment of buddhahood is his meaning, and he repeats, in a variety of forms, that a Buddha appears in the world in order that all living beings may apprehend and enter into "the Way of Buddha-knowledge", in other words, the mind and life of the Buddhas themselves. The Buddha can only teach his Way to bodhisattvas, that is, to those capable of receiving the higher Truth, so that they in turn may transmit it to all

68

the living. He teaches but one Way, one Vehicle; for a Hinayana, or Small Vehicle, is not big enough for his Truth, only the Mahayana can hold it. Only the Great Vehicle is capacious enough to hold all creatures. Such, he declares, is the Buddha-law taught in "countless hundreds, thousands, myriads, kotis of Buddha-lands in the universe". "All things are for the One Buddha-Vehicle, and living beings who hear the Law from the Buddhas, all finally obtain Perfect Enlightenment."

This is the fundamental revelation of the Sutra, repeated in a plenitude of language.

"I am also like the other Buddhas," he says. "Knowing that all the living have many and various desires deep-rooted in their minds, I have, according to their capacity, expounded the various laws (by which these could be overcome) with various reasonings, parabolic expressions, and expedients." But this tactical method was only in order to lead them onwards till they were capable of "attaining to the Perfect Knowledge of the One Buddha-Vehicle", for "in the whole universe there are not even two Vehicles, how much less a third". That is to say there are no two ways of salvation, none but that of the Mahayana.

He proceeds to say that a Buddha only appears in a period of decay, when "all the living are vile, covetous and envious, bringing to maturity every root of badness". Then a Buddha appears and, while still in the One Vehicle, expounds it as Three Vehicles. There is dispute as to the exact meaning

69

of the three, but they are understood as sravakas, pratyekabuddhas, and bodhisattvas, and these may be described as disciples still under the law of works, disciples who have accomplished their works, and Mahayana disciples who receive the true spiritual revelation in faith. If disciples of the first two types refuse to abandon their lower wisdom and the merits which they treasure, and to become bodhisattvas in the higher school, these can no longer be accounted faithful disciples.

This is repeated in many pages of verse, from which the following excerpts are taken:

"Monks and nuns
Obsessed by utmost arrogance,
Men-disciples in self-conceit,
Women-disciples in unbelief,
Such four groups as these
Five thousand in number,
Perceiving not their errors
And faults in the moral law,
Caring only for their flaws,
These little-wits having gone,
These husks of the assembly who withdraw
Because of the Buddha's majesty,
These men of minor virtues,
Unable to receive this Law—
(Now) has this assembly nor twigs nor leaves,
But only the true and real."

He proceeds to show how, by reading the hearts and lives, past, present, and future, of all men, he

adapts his teaching to their needs, telling them
stories, or poems, or transmigrations, or marvels,
and in parables leading them on.

> "The dull, who delight in petty rules,
> Who are greedily attached to mortality,
> Who have not, under countless Buddhas,
> Walked the profound and mystic Way,
> Who are harassed by all the sufferings—
> To these I (at first) preach Nirvana.
> Such is the expedient I employ
> To lead them to Buddha-wisdom.
> Not yet could I say to them,
> 'You all shall attain to Buddhahood',
> For the time had not yet arrived.
> But now the very time has come
> And I must preach the Great Vehicle."

He declares that the nine divisions of the Law,
which he had previously preached, were but the
approach to the Mahayana, and in it he assures
his bodhisattva-disciples of their ultimate buddhahood.

> "The Buddha appears in the world
> Only for this One Reality,
> The other two not being real;
> For never by a smaller Vehicle (Hinayana)
> (Could a Buddha) save any creature.
> The Buddha himself is in the Great-Vehicle
>   (Mahayana)
> And accordant with the Truth he has at-
>   tained,

71

Enriched by meditation and wisdom,
By it he saves all creatures.
I, having proved the Supreme Way,
The universality of the Great Vehicle,
If, by a Small Vehicle, I converted
Were it but one human being,
I should fall into grudging selfishness,
A thing that cannot be.
If men turn in faith to the Buddha,
The Tathagata will not deceive them,
Having no selfish, envious desires,
Being free from all sins of the Law.
Hence, the Buddha, in the universe,
Is the One being perfectly fearless."

In this passage we have clearly stated the distinctive character of Mahayana—its two prominent features of Universality and of Faith. The Buddha himself being universal, all beings must be included, for the whole contains its parts. The Supreme Way is Universalism and Faith in the sublime unselfishness of the Buddha.

It is quite apparent also that by the Buddha no merely human being is meant. A distinction is necessary between the earth-born Śakyamuni and the Buddha. As in the case of the divine-human nature of the Christ, so in regard to the Buddha, Śakyamuni is considered as a man who, when enlightened, became the human Buddha. His human nature had been clothed upon by the Buddha-nature. When on earth, though still human, the Buddha was more. He was even more than the highest devas, in other words more than the beings commonly called divine, for a Buddha, a truly enlightened one, was far greater than the passion-torn gods of India. However powerful and happy they may be as gods, they are still the subjects of mortality, and therefore of reincarnation, but from this a Buddha is free. In sum, the Buddha was in Śakyamuni reconciling all creatures unto himself, and thus Śakyamuni was Buddha. The Buddha is universal; therefore all things are in Buddha—and will be reconciled. But inferentially, as the Buddha has freedom of will, so all creatures have freedom of choice, and not till they choose to use their faculty of faith in the Buddha, rather than to use their own feeble efforts at enlightenment and moral control, will they reach the perfect enlightenment, in unity of spirit with the Buddha.

"Know, O Śariputra!
Of yore I made a vow,
In desire to cause all creatures
To rank equally with me.

. . . . . .

Whene'er I meet any of the living
I teach them the Buddha-Way;
The unwise remain confused
And, deluded, accept not my teaching."

The Buddha-Way is the way to buddhahood, or perfect enlightenment; the way is faith; the end is universal.

He proceeds to say:
"I know that all these creatures
Have failed in previous lives,
Are firmly attached to base desires
And, infatuated, are in trouble.

.   .   .   .   .

They suffer the utmost misery.
Received into the womb in embryo,
They pass from generation to generation,
Poor in virtue and of little happiness,
Oppressed by all the sorrows
And dwelling in the thickets of debate,
Such as, Existence? or Non-existence?
Relying on their propositions,
Sixty-two in number,
They become rooted in false philosophy,
Tenacious and unyielding,
Self-sufficient and self-inflated,
Suspicious, warped, without faith.
During thousands and milliards of kalpas
Such hear not the name of Buddha,
Nor ever learn of the Truth;
These men are hard to save.
For this reason, Śariputra,
I set up an expedient for them,
Proclaiming a Way to end suffering,
Revealing it as Nirvana.
Yet, though I proclaim Nirvana,
It is not real extinction;
All things from the beginning

74

Are ever of Nirvana nature.
When a Buddha-son fulfils (his) course,
In the world to come he becomes Buddha.
It is because of my adaptability
That I tell of a Three-Vehicle Law,
(But truly) the World-honoured Ones
Preach the One-Vehicle Way."

Thus the author declares that the ignorant, pre-
judiced, and warped condition of the human mind,
with its logic-chopping and philosophizing, only
leads men away from simple faith in the Buddha.
It is difficult to make them believe this, and only
by tactful, expedient teaching (i.e. Hinayana) can
men be led on to the truth as it is in Mahayana.
The other vehicles, or schools, are but temporary
expedients. The author, quite clearly, finds himself teaching a doctrine fundamentally different
from that which Śakyamuni had taught when on
earth, yet as he wishes to put the new teaching
into Śakyamuni's mouth, he has to justify the
change. In the meantime, he declares that, in all
past time and in all worlds, wherever the Buddhas
—before their final extinction from the lower
realms, before their final Nirvana, or blessedness—
have preached their Supreme Truth, the creatures
in each of their domains have been able to attain
to buddhahood:

"If there are any beings
Who have met the former Buddhas,
If, after hearing the Truth,
They have given kindly alms,

75

Or kept the commands, enduring,
Been zealous, meditative, wise,
Cultivating blessedness and virtue,
Such men and beings as these
Have all attained to buddhahood.
If, after the Nirvana of Buddhas,
Men have become gentle of heart,
All such creatures as these
Have all attained to buddhahood.
After the Nirvana of Buddhas,
Those who worshipped their relics,
And built myriads, kotis of stupas,
With gold, silver, and crystal,
With moonstone and with agate,
With jasper and lapis lazuli,
Purely and abundantly displayed,
Superbly shown on every stupa;
Or those who built shrines of stone,
Of sandal-wood or aloes,
Of eagle-wood or other woods,
Of brick and tiles, or clay;
Or those who, in the wilds,
Built Buddha-shrines of earth;
Even children who, in play,
Gathered sand for a Buddha's stupa;
Such men and beings as these,
Have all attained to buddhahood.
If men, for the sake of Buddhas,
Have erected images of them,
Carved with the (sacred) signs,
They have all attained to buddhahood."

4. Buddha accepts from a child a handful of dust with which it was
playing, all it had to give

In like manner those who have used brass, lead, clay, lacquer to make Buddha's images, or painted them, or employed others to do so, have also attained buddhahood.

"Even boys, in their play,
Who with reed, wood, or pen,
Or, even with finger-nail,
Have drawn Buddha's images;
Such men and beings as these
Gradually accumulating merit,
And becoming pitiful in heart,
Have all attained to buddhahood,
And converted many bodhisattvas,
Saving countless creatures."

Moreover:

"If men, to the stupas and shrines,
To a precious image or painting,
With flowers, incense, flags and umbrellas,
Have paid homage with respectful hearts;
Or employed others to perform music,
Beat drums, blow horns and conches,
Pan-pipes and flutes, play lutes and harps,
Gongs, guitars and cymbals,
Such mystic sounds as these,
Played by way of homage;
Or with joyful hearts have sung
Praise to the merits of Buddhas,
Though with but one small sound,
(These, too,) have attained to buddhahood.
Even one who, distracted of mind,

77

With but a single flower,
Has paid homage to a painted image,
Shall gradually see countless Buddhas.
Or, those who have offered worship,
Were it merely by folding the hands,
Or even by raising a hand,
Or by slightly bending the head,
By thus paying homage to the images,
Will gradually see countless Buddhas,
Attain the Supreme Way,
Widely save numberless creatures
And enter the perfect Nirvana.

.   .   .   .   .

(For) all Buddhas take the one vow:
'The Buddha-way which I walk,
I will universally cause all the living
To attain this same Way with me.'
Though Buddhas in future ages
Proclaim hundreds, thousands, kotis,
Countless ways into the doctrine,
In reality there is but the One-Vehicle.

.   .   .   .   .

In the perilous round of mortality,
In continuous, unending misery,
Firmly tied to the passions
As a yak is to its tail;
Smothered by greed and infatuation,
Blinded and seeing nothing;
Seeking not the Buddha, the Mighty,

And the Truth that ends suffering,
But deeply sunk in heresy,
By suffering seeking riddance of suffering;
For the sake of all these creatures
My heart is stirred with great pity."

The author then makes him refer to his enlightenment under the bodhi-tree, when the supreme
truth of Mahayanism is declared by the author to
have been revealed to him. So impossible did it
seem to Sakyamuni that the world could understand him, that he thought straightway to proclaim
the Mahayana Law once only, and immediately
betake himself to the bliss of Nirvana. But Brahma
and the gods and the heavenly throng earnestly
implored him not to leave the world, but to "roll
the Wheel of the Law", that is, proclaim the Good
News as the disk of the sun rolls through the sky.
Finally, he decides that, as it is impossible for
ignorant and sinful man immediately to apprehend
this wonderful Truth, it is needful for him to
use such tactful or Hinayana teaching as may be
expedient. Instantly the former Buddhas applaud
his decision, assuring him that such had been
their own method. Thus the Author gives him
the authority of the Buddhas of all past worlds.

"Know, Sariputra!
The stupid and those of little wit,
Those tied to externals and the proud,
Cannot believe this Truth.
But now I gladly and with boldness

79

In the midst of (you) bodhisattvas,
Straightway put aside expediency
And only proclaim the Supreme Way.

.   .   .   .   .

In the same fashion that the Buddhas,
Past, present, and future, preach the Law,
So also will I now proclaim
The one and undivided Law.

.   .   .   .   .

Even in infinite, countless kalpas,
Rarely may this Law be heard,
And those able to hearken to it,
Such men as these are rare.

.   .   .   .   .

Who hears and joyfully extols it,
Though but by a single word,
Has thus paid homage to
All Buddhas in the three realms.

.   .   .   .   .

Know, all of you, Śariputra,
That this Wonderful Law
Is the secret of all the Buddhas.

.   .   .   .   .

Rejoice greatly in your hearts,
Knowing that you will become Buddhas."

III

SARIPUTRA filled with a spirit of ecstasy, now addresses the Buddha, reproaching himself that he has heretofore struggled in the straits of the smaller vehicle, when, but for his own unbelief, he might have known the liberation of the Mahayana; as also might his fellow disciples.

"This is our fault, not the World-honoured One's. Wherefore? Because had we attended to his preaching in regard to Perfect Enlightenment, we should certainly have been delivered by the Great Vehicle. ... To-day I indeed know that I am really a son of Buddha, born from the mouth of Buddha, evolved from The Law, and have obtained a place in the Buddha-Law."

His address is again lengthily produced in verse:

> "Now I hear the voice of Buddha
> Opportunely preaching The Law,
> Faultless and inscrutable,
> By which all reach the Wisdom-throne."

.   .   .   .   .

In the former days he thought he had already reached the stage that brought Extinction (Nirvana);

> "But now I have perceived
> That was not real extinction.
> When one becomes a Buddha,

Complete with all the signs,
And devas, men and yakshas,
Nagas and spirits revere him,
Then that may be called
Eternal, complete extinction,
Without any remainder."

He means that he will attain to the eternal bliss of
the Buddhas without any remainder of reincarnation, or remainder of karma that requires reincarnation. He expresses a fear lest the wonderful
news he now hears might be the invention of the
devil; but he rejoices that this cannot be the case,
for—

"The World-honoured One preaches Truth,
Not so is it with the Evil One;
Henceforth I know for certain that
This is not Mara acting as Buddha.
'Twas through falling into nets of doubt,
I conceived it as the doing of Mara.
Now hearing Buddha's gentle voice,
Profound and most refined,
Expounding the pure Law,
My heart is filled with joy,
My doubts and regrets are ended
As I rest in real Wisdom,
Assured of becoming Buddha,
Revered by devas and men,
And, rolling the supreme Law-wheel,
Convert many bodhisattvas."

The Buddha then proceeds to tell them that this is

not the first world in which he has taught them. They have forgotten their previous incarnations; not so the Buddha. It is, indeed, because he has, in former incarnations, trained them that they are now born into his Law here. Then he foretells the future destiny of Śariputra, telling him he will be reborn as a prince, and like Sakyamuni leave his palace to become a monk.

"O son of Śari! In a world to come, after infinite, boundless, inconceivable kalpas, when you shall have served some thousands, myriads, kotis of Buddhas, maintained the Right Law, and completed the Way which Bodhisattvas walk, you shall become a Buddha, whose title will be Flower-light Tathagata, Worshipful, All-wise, Perfectly enlightened in conduct, Well-departed, Understander of the world, Peerless Leader, Controller, Teacher of gods and men, Buddha, World-honoured One, whose domain shall be named Undefiled, whose land will be even and straight, pure and adorned, peaceful and prosperous, filled with celestial people; the ground of lapis lazuli, having eight intersecting roads with golden cords to set bounds to their sides, flanked with trees of the Seven Precious things, always full of flowers and fruits. . . . Its kalpa will be named Jewel-adorned . . . for its bodhisattvas are its great jewels. These bodhisattvas will be infinite, boundless, inconceivable, beyond computation or compare, such as none can apprehend who has not a Buddha's wisdom. Wherever they walk jewel-flowers will receive their feet."

. . . . . .

"The Tathagata Flower-light, at the expiration of twelve minor kalpas, will predict the Bodhisattva 'Resolute' to Perfect Enlightenment and will declare to all the monks: 'This Bodhisattva Resolute will become the next Buddha, whose title will be Flowery-footsteps'."

.   .   .   .   .

"Sariputra! After the extinction of Flower-Light Buddha, the Correct Law will abide in his world during thirty-two minor kalpas, and then the Semblance Law will also abide in his world during thirty-two kalpas"; in other words, the usual formalism will set in, leading to decay and disappearance.

Then the monks and nuns, male and female disciples, gods, nagas, yakshas, gandharvas, asuras, garudas, kinnaras, mahoragas, and others, all the great assembly of beings, human and not human, rejoice greatly, each doffing his robe and offering it in homage to the Buddha. Brahma and the gods offer celestial robes and celestial flowers, their robes remaining aloft, circling around, while countless celestial instruments make music in the sky.

"Of old, at Varanasi, Thou didst roll
  The Law-wheel of the Four Noble Truths,
  And discerningly preach the Laws
  Of the rise and the extinction
  Of the Five human Aggregates.
  Now again Thou dost roll the most wonderful,

Mighty, Supreme, Wheel of the Law,
The Law beyond measure profound.

.   .   .   .   .

The great, wise Śariputra
Now has heard his prediction;
We also in like manner know
We too will become Buddhas,
Who in all worlds are ever
Most honoured and peerless."

Again the troublesome question is raised, why
the Buddha should have taught the Hinayana
doctrines, only now to repudiate them and offer
Mahayana doctrines in their stead. Śariputra says
that while he himself has no doubt or regrets, yet
here are twelve hundred disciples, "who of yore
abode in the four stages of (hinayana) learning, and
were always told by the Buddha—'My Law is able
to give freedom from re-birth, decrepitude, disease
and death and the final attainment of Nirvana'."
How is it that he now discards all this as valueless?
What becomes of the merit these disciples have
laid up with so much zeal and struggle? Has the
Buddha indeed been deceiving them is the meaning
of his inquiry.

To this the Buddha replies:

"Have I not before said that the Buddhas, the World-
honoured Ones, with a variety of reasonings, parables
and terms, preach the Law as may be expedient,
with the aim of final Perfect Enlightenment? All
their teachings are for the. purpose of transforming

(their disciples into) bodhisattvas. But, Śariputra!
Let me again in a parable make this meaning still
more clear, for intelligent people, through a parable,
reach understanding."

Parable of the Burning House.

"Śariputra! Suppose, in a (certain) kingdom, city,
or town, there is a great elder, old and worn, of
boundless wealth, and possessing many fields, houses,
slaves, and servants. His house is spacious and large,
but it has only one door, and many people dwell in it,
one hundred, two hundred, or even five hundred in
number. Its halls and chambers are decayed and old,
its walls crumbling down, the bases of its pillars
rotten, the beams and roof-trees toppling and dangerous. On every side, at the same moment, fire suddenly
starts and the house is in conflagration. The boys of
the elder, say ten, twenty, or even thirty, are in the
dwelling. The elder, on seeing this conflagration
spring up on every side, is greatly startled and reflects
thus: 'Though I am able to get safely out of the gate
of this burning house, yet my boys in the burning
house are pleasurably absorbed in amusements without apprehension, knowledge, surprise, or fear.
Though the fire is pressing upon them and pain and
suffering are instant, they do not mind or fear and
have no impulse to escape.'

"Śariputra! This elder ponders thus: 'I am strong
in my body and arms. Shall I get them out of the
house by means of a flower-vessel, or a bench, or a
table?' Again he ponders: 'This house has only one

86

gate, which moreover is narrow and small. My children are young, knowing nothing as yet and attached to their place of play; perchance they will fall into the fire and be burnt. I must speak to them on this dreadful matter (warning them) that the house is burning, and that they must come out instantly lest they are burnt and injured by the fire.' Having reflected thus, according to his thoughts, he calls to his children: 'Come out quickly, all of you!'

"Though their father, in his pity, lures and admonishes with kind words, yet the children, joyfully absorbed in their play, are unwilling to believe him and have neither surprise nor fear, nor any mind to escape; moreover, they do not know what is the fire (he means), or what the house, and what he means by being lost, but only run hither and thither in play, no more than glancing at their father. Then the elder reflects thus: 'This house is burning in a great conflagration. If I and my children do not get out at once, we shall certainly be burnt up by it. Let me now, by some expedient, cause my children to escape this disaster.' Knowing that to which each of his children is predisposed, and all the various attractive playthings and curiosities to which their natures will joyfully respond, the father tells them saying: '(Here are) rare and precious things for your amusement—if you do not (come) and get them, you will be sorry for it afterwards. So many goat-carts, deer-carts, and bullock-carts are now outside the gate to play with. All of you come quickly out of this burning house, and I will give you whatever you want.' Thereupon the children, hearing of the attractive playthings mentioned by their father, and because they suit their wishes, every one eagerly, each pushing the other, and racing one against another, comes rushing out of the burning house.

"Then the elder, seeing his children have safely escaped and are all in the square, sits down in the open, no longer embarrassed, but with a mind at ease and ecstatic with joy. Then each of the children says to the father: 'Father! Please now give us those playthings you promised us, goat-carts, deer-carts, and bullock-carts.' Sariputra! Then the elder gives to his children equally each a great cart, lofty and spacious, adorned with all the precious things, surrounded with railed seats, hung with bells on its four sides, and covered with curtains, splendidly decorated also with various rare and precious things, draped with strings of precious stones, hung with garlands of flowers, thickly spread with beautiful mats, and supplied with rosy pillows. It is yoked with white bullocks of pure (white) skin, of handsome appearance, and of great muscular power, which walk with even steps, and with the speed of the wind, and also has many servants and followers to guard them. Wherefore? Because this great elder is of boundless wealth and all his various store-houses are full to overflowing. So he reflects thus: 'My possessions being boundless, I must not give my children inferior small carts. All these children are my sons, whom I love without partiality. Having such great carts made of the seven precious things, infinite in number, I should with equal mind bestow them on each one without discrimination. Wherefore? Because, were I to give them to the whole nation, these things of mine would not run short—how much less so to my children! Meanwhile each of the children rides on his great cart, having received that which he had never before had and never expected to have.

"Śariputra! What is your opinion? Has that elder, in (only) giving great carts of the precious substances to his children equally, been in any way guilty of falsehood?"

"No, World-honoured One!" says Śariputra. "That elder only caused his children to escape the disaster of fire and preserved their bodies alive—he committed no falsity. Why? He thus preserved their bodies alive, and in addition gave them the playthings they obtained; moreover, it was by his expedient that he saved them from that burning house! World-honoured One! Even if that elder did not give them one of the smallest carts, still he is not false. Wherefore? Because that elder from the first formed this intention, 'I will, by an expedient, cause my children to escape'. For this reason he is not false. How much less so seeing that, knowing his own boundless wealth and desiring to benefit his children, he gives them great carts equally!"

"Good! Good!" replies the Buddha to Śariputra. "It is even as you say. Śariputra! The Tathagata is also like this, for he is the Father of all worlds, who has for ever entirely ended all fear, despondency, distress, ignorance, and enveloping darkness, and has perfected boundless knowledge, strength, and fear-lessness. He is possessed of great supernatural power and wisdom-power, has completely attained the Paramitas of adaptability and wisdom, and is the greatly merciful and greatly compassionate, ever tire-less, ever seeking the good, and benefiting all beings. He is born in this triple world, the old decayed burning house, to save all living creatures from the fires of birth, age, disease, death, grief, suffering, foolishness, darkness, and the Three Poisons, and teach them to obtain Perfect Enlightenment. He sees how all living creatures are scorched by the fires of birth, age, disease, death, grief, and sorrow, and suffer all kinds of distress by reason of the five desires and the greed of gain; and how, by reason of the attach-ments of desire and its pursuits, they now endure much suffering and hereafter will suffer in hell, or as animals or hungry spirits. Even if they are born in a heaven, or amongst men, there are all kinds of suffer-ings, such as the bitter straits of poverty, the bitterness of parting from loved ones, the bitterness of associa-tion with the detestable. Absorbed in these things, all living creatures rejoice and take their pleasure, while they neither apprehend, nor perceive, are neither alarmed, nor fear, and are without satiety, never seeking to escape, but, in the burning house of this triple world, running to and fro, and although they will meet with great suffering, count it not as cause for anxiety.

"Sariputra! The Buddha, having seen this, reflects thus: 'I am the Father of all creatures and must snatch them from suffering and give them the bliss of the infinite, boundless Buddha-wisdom for them to play with'.

"Śariputra! The Tathagata again reflects thus: 'If I only use supernatural power and wisdom, casting aside every tactful method, and extend to all living creatures the wisdom, power, and fearlessness of the Tathagata, the living creatures cannot by this method be saved. Wherefore? As long as all these creatures have not escaped birth, age, disease, death, grief, and suffering, but are being burnt in the burning house of the triple world, how can they understand the Buddha-wisdom?'

"Śariputra! Even as that elder, though with strength in body and arms, yet does not use it, but only by diligent tact, resolutely saves his children from the calamity of the burning house, and then gives each of them great carts adorned with precious things, so is it with the Tathagata. Though he has power and fearlessness, he does not use them, but only by his wise tact does he remove and save all living creatures from the burning house of the triple world, preaching the Three-Vehicles, viz. the Sravaka, Pratyekabuddha, and Buddha vehicles. And thus he speaks to them: 'Ye all! Delight not to dwell in the burning house of the triple world. Do not hanker after its crude forms, sounds, odours, flavours, and contacts. For if, through hankering, ye beget a love of it, then ye will be burnt by it. Get ye out with haste from the triple world and take to the Three-Vehicles, viz. the Sravaka, Pratyekabuddha, and Buddha

91

Vehicles. I now give you my pledge for this, and it will never prove false. Be only diligent and zealous!' By these expedients does the Tathagata lure all creatures forth, and again speaks thus: 'Know ye! All these Three-Vehicles are praised by sages: in them you will be free and independent, without wanting to rely on aught else. Riding in these Three Vehicles, by means of perfect faculties, powers, perceptions, ways, concentrations, emancipations, and samadhis, ye will, as a matter of course, be happy and gain infinite peace and joy.'

"Sariputra! If there are living beings who have a spirit of wisdom within and, following the Buddha, the World-honoured One, hear the Law, receive it in faith, and zealously make progress, desiring speedily to escape from the triple world and seeking Nirvana for themselves—this (type) is called the Sravaka-Vehicle, just as some of those children come out of the burning house for the sake of a goat-cart. If there are living beings who, following the Buddha, the World-honoured One, hear the Law, receive it in faith, and zealously make progress, seeking self-gained Wisdom, taking pleasure in becoming good and calm, and deeply versed in the causes and reasons of the laws—this type is called the Pratyekabuddha-Vehicle, just as some of those children come out of the burning house for the sake of a deer-cart. If there are living beings who, following the Buddha, the World-honoured One, hear the Law, receive it in faith, diligently practise and zealously advance, seeking the Complete Wisdom, Buddha-Wisdom, the

Natural Wisdom, the Masterless Wisdom, and Tathagata knowledge, powers, and fearlessness, who take pity on and comfort innumerable creatures, benefit devas and men, and save all beings—this type is called the Great-Vehicle. Because bodhisattvas seek this vehicle, they are named mahasattvas. They are like those children who come out of the burning house for the sake of a bullock-cart.

"Sariputra! Just as that elder, seeing his children get out of the burning house safely to a place free from fear, and pondering on his immeasurable wealth, gives each of his children a great cart, so also is it with the Tathagata. Being the Father of all living creatures, if he sees infinite thousands of kotis of creatures, by the teaching of the Buddha, escape from the suffering of the triple world, from fearful and perilous paths, and gain the joys of Nirvana, the Tathagata then reflects thus: 'I possess infinite, boundless wisdom, power, fearlessness, and other Law-treasuries of Buddhas. All these living creatures are my children to whom I will equally give the Great-Vehicle, so that none will gain an individual Nirvana, but all gain Nirvana by the same Nirvana as the Tathagata. All these living creatures who escape the triple world are given the playthings of Buddhas, viz. concentrations, emancipations, and so forth, all of the same pattern and of one kind, praised by sages and able to produce pure, supreme pleasure.

"Sariputra! Even as that elder at first attracted his children by the three carts, and afterwards gave them only a great cart magnificently adorned with precious

things and supremely comfortable, yet that elder is
not guilty of falsehood, so also is it with the Tathagata; there is no falsehood in first preaching Three-
Vehicles to attract all living creatures and afterwards
in saving them by the Great Vehicle only. Wherefore? Because the Tathagata possesses infinite wisdom, power, fearlessness, and the treasury of the laws,
and is able to give all living creatures the Great
Vehicle Law; but not all are able to receive it. Sariputra! For this reason know that Buddhas, by their
adaptability, in the One Buddha-Vehicle define and
expound the Three."

The embellishment in the verse section will be
seen in the following example:

"Suppose, there is an elder,
Who has a large house,
A house for long old,
And falling in decay;
Its lofty halls are tottering,
The pillar-bases rotting,
Beams and roof-trees toppling,
Foundations all collapsing,
Walls and partitions in ruins,
Their plaster crumbling away,
Thatch disordered and dropping,
Rafters awry and falling,
Fences bent and distorted,
Behind them a fullness of refuse;
Five hundred individuals
Are dwelling there within it.

Owls, hawks, and vultures,
Crows, magpies, pigeons, doves,
Black snakes, vipers, scorpions,
Centipedes and millipedes,
Geckos, galley-worms,
Weasels, ferrets, rats, and mice,
All sorts of evil creatures,
Run about in every direction;
Places stink with excrement,
Overflowing with uncleanness;
Dung-beetles and worms
Flock together in them.
Foxes, wolves, and jackals
Bite and trample each other
To gnaw human carcasses,
Scattering their bones and flesh.
Following these, troops of dogs
Come striving to snatch and grab,
And, gaunt with hunger, skulk about
Everywhere seeking food,
Quarrelling and scuffling,
Snarling and loud-barking.
Such is that house's fearfulness
And its changed character.
  Everywhere there are
Hobgoblins and ogres,
Yakshas and malign demons,
Who devour the flesh of men;
All sorts of venomous insects,
And evil birds and brutes
Hatch or suckle their broods,

Each hiding and guarding its own;
Yakshas come striving together,
To seize and eat them for food;
Having eaten their fill,
Their evil minds are inflamed,
And the sound of their wrangling
Stirs to utmost fear.
Kumbhanda-demons also
Crouch upon the mounds,
Springing from the ground
A foot or two feet high,
Wandering about to and fro,
Giving full rein to their tricks;
Seizing dogs by their feet,
Beating them to silence,
Throwing their legs over their necks,
Scaring them for amusement.
   Also there are demons,
Of stature tall and large,
Naked, black, and lean,
Who always dwell therein,
Emitting horrible sounds,
Bellowing in search of food.
Again there are demons
With throats narrow as a needle.
And there are also demons,
With heads like a bullock's;
Some which eat human flesh,
Others which devour dogs,
Their locks are dishevelled,
They are cruel and fiendish,

Oppressed by hunger and thirst,
They rush about crying and calling.
Yakshas and hungry ghosts,
Evil birds and beasts
Hungrily hurry in all directions,
Peeping through window and lattice.
Such are its plagues,
Fearful beyond measure."

The author further defends the Buddha for his
method of expediency in the following lines:

"Though Buddhas, the World-honoured,
Convert by expedient methods,
Yet the living they convert
Are indeed all bodhisattvas.
To such as are of little wit,
Deeply attached to desire and passion,
The Buddha, for their sake,
Preaches the Truth about Suffering,
And all the living joyfully
Attain the unprecedented.
The Buddha's Truth about Suffering,
Is real without distinction.
Those living beings who
Know not the root of suffering,
Cling to the cause of suffering,
Unable to leave it a moment.
Again, for the sake of these,
He preaches the Truth with tact (saying):
'The cause of all suffering
Is rooted in desire.'

If desire be extinguished,
Suffering has no foothold.
To annihilate suffering
Is called the Third Truth.
For the sake of the Truth of Extinction,
To cultivate oneself in the Way,
Forsaking all ties to suffering,
This is called Emancipation.
From what then have these people
Attained Emancipation?
Merely to depart from the false
They call Emancipation;
But in truth that is not yet
Complete Emancipation.
   So Buddha declares: These people
Have not reached real extinction;
Because these people have not yet
Gained the Supreme Way,
I am unwilling to declare
That they have attained extinction.
I am the King of the Law,
Absolute in regard to the Law,
For comforting all creatures
I appear in the world.
   Śariputra! This,
My final Seal of the Law,
Because of my desire to benefit
All the world, is now announced;
Wherever you may wander,
Do not carelessly proclaim it.
If there be hearers who joyfully

Receive it with deep obeisance,
You may know those people
Are Avinivartaniyah.
If there be any who receive
This Sutra-Law in faith,
These people must already
Have seen Buddhas of past times,
Revered and worshipped them
And listened to this Law.
If there be any who are able
To believe in your preaching,
They must formerly have seen me,
And also have seen you,
And these bhikshu-monks,
As well as these bodhisattvas.
    This Law-Flower Sutra
Is addressed to the truly wise;
Men shallow of knowledge hearing it,
Go astray not understanding.
All the Sravakas,
And Pratyekabuddhas,
Cannot by their powers
Attain unto this Sutra.
Sariputra!
Even you, into this Sutra
Enter only by faith,
Much more must the other Sravakas.
The other Sravakas,
By believing the Buddha's words,
Obediently follow this Sutra,
Not by wisdom they have of their own."

The terrible consequences of contemning the
Mahayana, as offered by The Lotus Sutra, are
shown thus:

"Again, Sariputra!
To the haughty and indifferent
And those with self-centred views,
Do not preach this Sutra.
To common shallow people,
Deeply attached to the five desires,
Who hear but cannot apprehend,
Do not preach it to them.
If such people do not believe in,
But vilify this Sutra,
They cut themselves off from all
The Buddha-Seed in the world;
Or if, sullenly frowning,
They are harbourers of doubts,
Listen to my declaration on the
Recompense of their sin:
'Whether during the Buddha's lifetime,
Or after his extinction,
If there be any who slander
A Sutra such as this,
Who, seeing those who read, recite,
Write or hold this Sutra,
Despise, scorn, hate, or envy them
And cherish tenacious grudge;
To the ill reward of such,
Listen now again;
After their lifetime's end,
They will enter the Avici-hell,

For a complete kalpa;
Reborn at each kalpa's end,
They thus go on revolving
Unto innumerable kalpas;
When they come out of hell,
They will degrade into animals,
Such as dogs or jackals,
With lean-cheeked forms,
Blue-black with scabs and sores,
The sport of men;
Moreover by men
Hated and scorned,
Ever suffering hunger and thirst,
Bones and flesh withered up.
Alive, beaten with thorns,
Dead, with shards and stones;
By cutting themselves off from the Buddha-
    seed,
They receive such recompense.
   Perhaps they become camels,
Or are born amongst asses,
Always carrying burdens,
Beaten and driven with sticks,
Thinking only of water and grass,
Knowing nothing else;
For slandering this Sutra,
Such is their punishment.
Some who become jackals,
Enter into a village,
Their bodies scabbed with sores,
Without even one whole eye,

By all the village boys
They are beaten and stoned,
Suffering bitter pains,
At times even to death.
When they have thus died,
Each receives a snake's body,
Of shape as long as
Five hundred yojanas;
Deaf and stupid, without feet,
They wriggle about on their bellies,
By many kinds of insects
Stung and devoured,
Day and night in misery
Without cessation;
Because of slandering this Sutra,
Such is their punishment.
    Should they become human beings,
Their natural powers are dull;
Dwarfed, ugly, palsied, and lame,
Blind, deaf, and humpbacked;
Whatever they say,
No one believes;
Their breath is vile,
They are demon-possessed,
They are needy and menial,
Ordered about by others,
Often ill and emaciated,
Having none on whom to rely;
Even those on whom they depend
Take no notice of them;
If they should get anything,

It is speedily forgotten;
If they practise means of healing
And follow the usual treatment,
Other ailments will be added,
Or, their patients will die;
If they themselves are ill,
None will save and cure them;
Though they take the best medicine,
They only grow worse.
Though it is others who run riot,
Pillaging and plundering,
For such crimes as these
On them falls perverse retribution.
   Such sinners as these
Never see the Buddha,
The King of Sages,
Preaching the Law and transforming;
Such sinners as these
Are always born in distress;
Mad, deaf, and confused in mind,
They never hear the Law;
During kalpas innumerable
As the sands of Ganges,
In life they are deaf and dumb,
With deficient natural powers;
They ever dwell in the hells
As their only pleasure gardens;
Or in other evil states,
As their dwelling-places;
Among asses, hogs, and dogs,
Are the places to which they go;

Because of slandering this Sutra,
Such is their punishment.
If they become human beings,
They are deaf, blind, and dumb,
Poor, needy, and feeble,
For their adornment
Dropsy and scurf,
Scab, sore, and abscess,
All such ills as these
Are their apparel.
Their bodies are foetid abodes,
Filthy and unclean;
Deeply absorbed in themselves,
They swell with anger,
Carnal passions inflame them,
No better are they than beasts;
Because of slandering this Sutra,
Such is their punishment.'
    I say to you, Śariputra!
Those who slander this Sutra,
To tell the tale of their evils,
A whole kalpa would not suffice.
For this cause and reason
I especially say to you:
'Among unwise people,
Do not preach this Sutra'."

Following this is a long account of those to whom
The Lotus may be preached; that is, to those who
have understanding, are true seekers of Buddhahood, unselfish, have left all, are reverent, upright,
patient, compassionate, and in general the sincere

humble seeker, who refuses all substitutes, such as other sutras, books, and philosophies.

> "I say to you, Śariputra,
> Were I to detail all the kinds
> Of seekers of the Buddhahood
> I could not finish in a kalpa.
> Such people as these are able
> To believe and to discern.
> Preach then to such as these
> The Wonderful Law-Flower Sutra."

IV

FROM among the throng on the stage of the Spiritual Vulture Peak, four of the oldest disciples of Śakyamuni are now seen to approach the Master. They come to say that, having fulfilled all the course previously laid down by him, they considered they had reached the stage of Nirvana; old and worn out they had not realized the possibility of a still higher bodhisattva state with its supernal joys. Now, hearing it so wonderfully portrayed, despite their advanced years they are filled with delight and longing.

At the prospect of Perfect Enlightenment they rejoice, and ask permission to make their meaning clear in a parable. This may be styled the Buddhist parable of the Prodigal Son, though it might even more correctly be called the parable of the Seeking Father. In it appears another defence of the Buddha's tactical method of teaching.

The Prodigal Son and the Seeking Father.

"It is like a youth who, on attaining manhood, leaves his father and runs away. For long he dwells in some other country, ten, twenty, or fifty years. The older he grows, the more needy he becomes. Roaming about in all directions to seek clothing and food, he gradually wanders along till he unexpectedly approaches his native country. From the first the father searched for his son but in vain, and meanwhile has settled in a certain city. His home becomes very rich; his goods and treasures are incalculable; gold, silver, lapis lazuli, corals, amber, crystal, and other gems so increase that his treasuries overflow; many youths and slaves has he, retainers and attendants, and countless elephants, horses, carriages, animals to ride, and kine and sheep. His revenues and investments spread to other countries, and his traders and customers are many in the extreme.

"At this time, the poor son, wandering through village after village, and passing through countries and cities, at last reaches the city where his father has settled. Always has the father been thinking of his son, yet, though he has been parted from him over fifty years, he has never spoken of the matter to any one, only pondering over it within himself and cherishing regret in his heart, as he reflects: 'Old and worn, I own much wealth; gold, silver, and jewels, granaries and treasuries overflowing; but I have no son. Some day my end will come and my wealth be scattered and lost, for there is no one to whom I can leave it.' Thus does he often think of his son, and earnestly repeats this reflection: 'If I could only get back my son and commit my wealth to him, how contented and happy should I be, with never a further anxiety!'

"World-honoured One! Meanwhile the poor son, hired for wages here and there, unexpectedly arrives at his father's house. Standing by the gate, he sees from afar his father seated on a lion-couch, his feet on a jewelled footstool, revered and surrounded by brahmanas, kshatriyas, and citizens, and with strings of pearls, worth thousands and myriads, adorning his body; attendants and young slaves with white chowries wait upon him right and left; he is covered by a rich canopy from which hang streamers of flowers; perfume is sprinkled on the earth, all kinds of famous flowers are scattered around, and precious things are placed in rows for his acceptance or rejection. Such is his glory, and the honour of his dignity. The poor son, seeing his father possessed of such great power, is seized with fear, regretting that he has come to this place, and secretly reflects thus: 'This must be a king, or some one of royal rank; it is no place for me to obtain anything for the hire of my labour. I had better go to some poor hamlet, where there is a place for letting out my labour, and food and clothing are easier to get. If I tarry here long, I may suffer oppression and forced service.'

"Having reflected thus, he hastens away. Meanwhile, the rich elder on his lion-seat has recognized his son at first sight, and with great joy in his heart has also reflected: 'Now I have some one to whom my treasuries of wealth are to be made over. Always have I been thinking of this my son, with no means of seeing him; but suddenly he himself has come and my longing is satisfied. Though worn with years, I yearn for him as of old.'

"Instantly he dispatches his attendants to pursue him quickly and fetch him back. Thereupon the messengers hasten forth to seize him. The poor son, surprised and scared, loudly cries his complaint:

'I have committed no offence against you; why should I be arrested?' The messengers all the more hasten to lay hold of him and compel him to go back. Thereupon, the poor son, thinking within himself that though he is innocent yet he will be imprisoned, and that now he will surely die, is all the more terrified, faints away and falls prostrate on the ground. The father, seeing this from afar, sends word to the messengers: 'I have no need for this man. Do not bring him by force. Sprinkle cold water on his face to restore him to consciousness and do not speak to him any further.' Wherefore? The father, knowing that his son's disposition is inferior, knowing that his own lordly position has caused distress to his son, yet convinced that he is his son, tactfully does not say to others: 'This is my son.'

A messenger says to the son: 'I now set you free; go wherever you will.' The poor son is delighted, thus obtaining the unexpected. He rises from the ground and goes to a poor hamlet in search of food and clothing. Then the elder, desiring to attract his son, sets up a device. Secretly he sends two men, doleful and shabby in appearance, saying—'You go and visit that place and gently say to the poor man—"There is a place for you to work here; you will be given double wages." If the poor man agrees, bring him back and give him work. If he asks what work you wish him to do, then you may say to him—"We will hire you for scavenging, and we both also will work along with you".' Then the two messengers go in search of the poor son and, having found him, place before him the above proposal. Thereupon the poor son, having received his wages beforehand, joins with them in removing a dirt-heap.

His father, beholding the son, is struck with compassion for, and wonder at, him. Another day he sees at a distance, through a window, his son's figure, gaunt, lean, and doleful, filthy and unclean with dirt and dust; thereupon he takes off his strings of jewels, his soft attire, and ornaments, and puts on a coarse, torn, and dirty garment, smears his body with dust, takes a dust-hod in his right hand, and with an appearance fear-inspiring says to the labourers: 'Get on with your work, don't be lazy.' By such a device he gets near to his son, to whom he afterwards says: 'Ay, my man, you stay and work here, do not go again elsewhere; I will increase your wages; give whatever you need, bowls, utensils, rice, wheat-flour, salt, vinegar and so on; have no hesitation; besides there is an old and worn-out servant whom you shall be given if you need him. Be at ease in your mind; I am, as it were, your father; do not be worried again. Wherefore? I am old and advanced in years, but you are young and vigorous; all the time you have been working, you have never been deceitful, lazy, angry or grumbling; I have never seen you, like the other labourers, with such vices as these. From this time forth you shall be as my own begotten son.'

"Thereupon the elder gives him a new name and calls him a son. The poor son, though he rejoices at this happening, still thinks of himself as a humble hireling. For this reason, during twenty years he continues to be employed in scavenging. After this period, there grows mutual confidence between them, and he goes in and out and is at his ease, though his abode is still the original place.

"World-honoured One! Then the elder becomes ill and, knowing that he will die before long, says to the poor son: 'Now I possess abundance of gold, silver, and precious things, and my granaries and treasuries are full to overflowing. The quantities of these things, and the amounts which should be received and given, I want you to understand in detail. Such is my mind, and you must agree to this my wish. Wherefore? Because, now, I and you are of the same mind. Be increasingly careful so that there be no waste.'

"The poor son accepts his instruction and commands, and becomes acquainted with all the goods, gold, silver, and precious things, as well as all the granaries and treasuries, but has no idea of expecting to inherit so much as a meal, while his abode is still the .original place and he is yet unable to abandon his sense of inferiority.

"After a short time has again passed, the father, knowing that his son's ideas have gradually been enlarged, his aspirations developed, and that he despises his previous state of mind, on seeing that his own end is approaching, commands his son to come, and gathers together his relatives, and the kings, ministers, kshatriyas, and citizens. When they are all assembled, he thereupon addresses them saying: 'Now, gentlemen, this is my son, begotten by me. It is over fifty years since, from a certain city, he left me and ran away to endure loneliness and misery. His former name was so-and-so and my name was so-and-so. At that time in that city I sought him sorrowfully. Suddenly in this place I met and regained him. This is really my son and I am really his father. Now all the wealth which I possess entirely belongs to my son, and all my previous disbursements and receipts are known by this son.'

"World-honoured One! When the poor son heard these words of his father, great was his joy at such unexpected news, and thus he thought: 'Without any mind for, or effort on my part, these treasures now come of themselves to me.'

"World-honoured One! The very rich elder is the Tathagata, and we are all as the Buddha's sons. The Tathagata has always declared that we are his sons. World-honoured One! Because of the three sufferings, in the midst of births-and-deaths we have borne all kinds of torments, being deluded and ignorant and enjoying our attachment to trifles. To-day the World-honoured One has caused us to ponder over and remove the dirt of all diverting discussions of inferior things. In these we have hitherto been diligent to make progress and have got, as it were, a day's pay for our effort to reach Nirvana. Obtaining this, we greatly rejoiced and were contented, saying to ourselves: 'For our diligence and progress in the Buddha-law what we have received is ample.' But the World-honoured One, knowing beforehand that our minds were attached to low desires and took delight in inferior things, let us go our own way, and did not dis-

criminate for us, saying: 'You shall yet have possession of the treasury of Tathagata-knowledge.' The
World-honoured One, in his tactfulness, told of the
Tathagata-wisdom ; but we, though following the
Buddha and receiving a day's wage of Nirvana,
deemed this a sufficient gain, never having a mind to
seek after the Great-Vehicle. We, also, have declared
and expounded the Tathagata-wisdom to bodhisattvas,
but in regard to this Great-Vehicle we have never had
a longing for it. Wherefore? The Buddha, knowing
that our minds delighted in inferior things, by his tactfulness taught according to our capacity, but still we
did not perceive that we were really Buddha-sons.

"Now we have just realized that the World-
honoured One does not grudge even the Buddha-
wisdom. Wherefore? From of old we are really
sons of Buddha, but have only taken pleasure
in minor matters; if we had had a mind to take
pleasure in the Great, the Buddha would have
preached the Great Vehicle Law to us. At length, in
this Sutra, he preaches only the One-Vehicle; and
though formerly, in the presence of bodhisattvas, he
spoke disparagingly of sravakas who were pleased
with minor matters, yet the Buddha had in reality
been instructing them in the Great-Vehicle. Therefore we say that though we had no mind to hope or
expect it, yet now the Great Treasure of the King of
the Law has of itself come to us, and such things as
Buddha-sons should obtain, we have all obtained."

The lengthy version in verse, while faithful to the
ideas of the prose section, is interesting for the

further detail it gives. For instance, the description
of the father's wealth:

"Very rich is his house,
Abundance of silver and gold,
Moonstones and agates,
Pearls and lapis lazuli,
Elephants, horses, oxen, and sheep,
Palanquins, litters, carriages,
Husbandmen, young slaves,
And a multitude of people;
His revenues and investments
Spread even to other countries;
His traders and his customers
Are everywhere to be found;
Thousands, myriads, kotis of people
Surround and honour him;
Constantly by the king
He is held in affection;
The ministers and noble families
Honour him most highly;
For all these reasons
His guests are many;
Such is the abundance of his wealth,
And the greatness of his power.
But his years are wearing away
And he mourns the more his son;
Morning and night he ponders:
'The time of my death is approaching;
My foolish son has left me
For over fifty years;
The things in my storehouses—

What shall I do with them?'
   At that time the poor son
Was seeking food and clothing
From city on to city.
From country on to country,
Sometimes getting something,
Sometimes finding nothing;
Famished, weak and gaunt,
Covered with scab and itch,
Gradually he passes along
To the city where dwells his father.
Hired for wages he roams,
At last reaching his father's house.
At that very hour the elder,
Within his gate, has set up
A great costly canopy,
And sits on a lion-seat,
Surrounded by his attendants,
Every one caring for him,
Some are counting up
Gold, silver, and precious things;
Incoming and outgoing goods,
Noting and recording bonds.
   The poor son, seeing his father
So noble, honoured and splendid,
Thinks: 'This must be a king
Or one of royal rank.'
Alarmed and wondering, he says:
'Why have I come here?'
Again he thinks to himself,
'If I tarry here long,

I may suffer oppression
And be driven to forced labour.'
Having pondered thus,
He hurries away in haste
To seek some poorer place,
That he may hire his labour.

   At that very time the elder,
Seated on the lion-seat,
Seeing his son from afar,
Secretly recognizes him,
And instantly orders servants
To pursue and fetch him back.
The poor son cries in alarm,
Faints and falls on the ground:
'Ah! These men have caught me;
I shall certainly be killed;
Why did food and clothing,
Cause me to come here?'

   The elder, knowing that his son.
Being foolish and inferior,
Will not believe in his word,
Nor believe he is his father,
With tactful method then
Again dispatches others,
One-eyed, squat, and common,
And unimposing, bidding them:
'Go and tell him saying,
'You be hired with us
To remove dirt and rubbish
And you shall have double wages.'
The poor son hearing this

Is glad, and comes with them,
For the purpose of moving dirt
And also cleansing outhouses.
  The elder, through a lattice,
Constantly sees his son,
And thinks of him as simple
And pleased with humble things.
Thereupon the elder,
Donning a tattered garment,
Taking along a dirt-hod,
Goes to where his son is;
By this device he gets near him,
Bidding him be diligent:
'I have decided to raise your wages,
And give you oil for your feet,
And plenty of food and drink,
And also thick warm mats.'
With sharp words he thus chides:
'Get you on with the work.'
Again he speaks gently:
'You are as it were my son.'
The elder, being wise,
Gradually has him go in and out,
And after twenty years,
Employs him as his steward,
Showing him his gold and silver,
His pearls and his crystal,
And the income and outgo of things,
All these he makes him know."

The scene opens, as already shown, with the approach to the Buddha of the elders, who tell the

parable given above and now close, in the verse
section, as follows:

"We all, during a long night-time,
Neither coveted nor were allied
To the true Buddha-wisdom,
Nor had aspiration to it.
For we, in regard to the Law
Thought we had reached finality.
We, for a long night-time,
Keeping the law of the Void,
Escaped from the triple world's
Harassing distresses,
And dwelt in the last bodily stage
Of Nirvana, where form only remains.
Taught by the Buddha we thought
We had attained, without doubt, the Way,
And that we had thereby
Repaid the Buddha's grace.

.   .   .   .

But in the law of bodhisattva
We never had wish nor pleasure.
Our Leader saw and let us be,
For he looked into our minds,
And at first stirred not our zeal
By telling of the true Gain.
Just as the rich elder,
Knowing his son's lower bent,
By his own tactfulness,
Moulds and subdues his mind,
And, only after that, gives him

118

The whole of his riches.
So is it with the Buddha
In the display of his rarities;
Knowing those pleased with trifles,
Yet by his tactfulness
He subdues their minds,
And teaches them the greater wisdom.
To-day we have obtained
What we never had before;
What we previously never looked for
We have unforeseen obtained,
Just as that poor son
Obtained inestimable treasures.

    World-honoured One! Now we
Have got the Way and the Fruit,
And, in the faultless Law,
Attained to clear vision.
For long time have we kept
The Buddha's pure commands,
To-day for the first time
We obtain its fruit and reward.
In the Law of the Law-King,
Having long practised arya deeds,
Now we attain the faultless,
Peerless great Fruit.
Now at last we are
Really hearers of the Sound,
Who take the news of Buddhahood
And make all creatures hear.
Now at last we are
Really Arahats,

Who, in all the worlds of
Gods, men, maras, and brahmans,
Universally by them
Are worthy of worship.
    The World-honoured One, in great grace,
With rare and precious things,
Compassionates, instructs
And confers benefits on us;
Through countless kotis of kalpas,
Who could ever repay him?
Service of hands and feet,
Homage all prostrate,
Every kind of offering,
Are all unable to repay.
If one bore him on one's head,
Or carried him on one's shoulders,
Through kalpas as the sands of Ganges,
Revering him with the whole mind;
Or with the best of food,
Countless costly garments,
And all kinds of bed-things;
Or every sort of medicament;
Or, with Ox-head sandal-wood
And all kinds of jewels,
Erect stupas and monasteries,
Or carpet the ground with costly robes;
With such things as these,
To pay him homage
Through kalpas as sands of Ganges,
One still could not repay.
Buddhas, with their rare,

Infinite and boundless,
Inconceivably great
Powers transcendent,
Faultless and effortless,
Kings of the Law,
Are able, for inferior minds,
In this matter to be patient,
And, for common folk attached to externals,
To preach as may befit them.
Buddhas, in the Law,
Attain to supreme power,
Know all living beings,
With their desires and pleasures,
And their aspirations,
So, according to their capacity,
By innumerable parables,
To them they preach the Law.
According as all the living
Have in past lives planted good roots,
The Buddhas, discerning the mature
From the immature,
And taking account of each,
Discriminating and understanding,
As may be most befitting
In the One Vehicle preach the Three."

V

THE Buddha now praises the four elders for their discernment, but adds that the Tathagata has numberless other qualities, which could not be told if enumerated for infinite kotis of kalpas.

"Know, Kaśyapa! The Tathagata is the King of the Laws (i. e. the King of all things). Whatever he says is entirely free from falsity. He explains all laws (or things) by wise tactfulness. The laws preached by him have Perfect Enlightenment as their aim. The Tathagata sees and knows what is the goal of all laws, and also knows what all living beings in their inmost hearts are doing, penetrating them without hindrance. Moreover, in regard to all laws, having the utmost understanding of them, he reveals to the living the wisdom of Perfect Enlightenment.

"Kaśyapa! Suppose, in a Three-Thousand-Great-Thousandfold-World (or chiliocosm), there are growing, on the mountains, along the rivers and streams, in the valleys and on the lands, plants, trees, thickets, forests, and medicinal herbs, of various and numerous kinds, with names and forms all different. A dense cloud spreads over and everywhere covers the whole Three-Thousand-Great-Thousandfold-World, and pours down its rain equally at the same time. Its moisture universally fertilizes the plants, trees, thickets, forests and medicinal herbs, with their tiny roots, tiny stalks, tiny twigs, tiny leaves; their medium roots, medium stalks, medium twigs, medium

5. Buddha divides the swollen torrent and walks over dryshod

leaves; their big roots, big stalks, big twigs, and big leaves; every tree, big or little, according to its superior, middle or lower capacity, receives its share. From the rain of the one cloud, each according to its species acquires its growth and the profusion of its flowers and fruit. Though produced in the same soil and moistened by the same rain, yet these plants and trees are all different.

"Know, Kaśyapa! The Tathagata is also like this; He appears in the world like the rising of a great cloud, with a great sound universally extending over the world of gods, men, and asuras, just as that great cloud everywhere covers the Three-Thousand-Great-Thousandfold-Region. In the great assembly he chants forth these words: 'I am the Tathagata, the Worshipful, the All Wise, of Perfectly Enlightened Conduct, the Well-Departed, the Understander of the World, the Peerless Leader, the Controller, the Teacher of gods and men, the Buddha, the World-honoured One. Those who have not yet been saved I cause to be saved; those who have not yet been set free to be set free; those who have not yet been comforted to be comforted; those who have not yet obtained nirvana to obtain nirvana. I know the present world and the world to come, as they really are. I am the All-knowing, the All-seeing, the Knower of the Way, the Opener of the Way, the Preacher of the Way. Come to me, all ye gods, men, and asuras, to hear the Law.' Then, numberless thousands, myriads, kotis of classes of living beings come to the Buddha to hear the Law. Thereupon the Tathagata, observing the natural powers of these beings, keen or dull, zealous or indifferent, according to their capacity preaches to them the Law in varying and unstinted ways, causing them to rejoice and joyfully to obtain much profit. All those living beings, on hearing this Law, are comforted in the present life and afterwards will be born in happy states, made joyful by the Truth, and will also hear the Law. Having heard the Law, they are freed from hindrances and, according to their capacity in the laws, they gradually enter the Way.

"Just as that great cloud, raining on all the plants, trees, thickets, forests, and medicinal herbs, and according to the nature of their seed perfectly fertilizes them, so that each grows and develops, in like manner the Law preached by the Tathagata is of one form and one flavour, that is to say, Deliverance, Abandonment, Extinction, and finally the attainment of Perfect Knowledge. If there be living beings who hear the Law of the Tathagata and keep, read, recite and practise it as preached, their achievements will not give them self-knowledge. Wherefore? Because there is only the Tathagata who knows the Seed, the Form, the Embodiment, and the Nature of all these living beings, what things they are reflecting upon, what things they are thinking, what things practising, how reflecting, how thinking, how practising, by what method reflecting, by what method thinking, by what method practising, and by what laws attaining to what laws. There is only the Tathagata who in reality sees, clearly and without hindrance, the varying stages in which all living beings are. It is like those plants, trees, thickets, forests, medicinal herbs, and others which do not know their own natures, superior, middle, or inferior. The Tathagata knows this unitary essential Law, that is to say, Deliverance, Abandonment, Extinction, final Nirvana of eternal rest, ending in return to the Void. The Buddha, knowing this and observing the disposition of all living beings, carefully leads them on. For this reason He does not immediately declare to them the complete and perfect wisdom. Kasyapa! All of you! A most rare thing it is that you should be able to know the Law preached by the Tathagata as he sees fit, and be able to believe and to receive it. Wherefore? Because the Law preached by Buddhas, the World-honoured Ones, as they see fit, is difficult to discern and difficult to know."

The following are selections from the section in verse:

"Know, Kaśyapa!
It is like unto a great cloud
Rising above the world,
Covering all things everywhere,
A gracious cloud full of moisture;
Lightning-flames flash and dazzle,
Voice of thunder vibrates afar,
Bringing joy and ease to all.
The sun's rays are veiled,
And the earth is cooled;
The cloud lowers and spreads
As if it might be caught and gathered;

Its rain everywhere equally
Descends on all sides,
Streaming and pouring unstinted,
Permeating the land.
On mountains, by rivers, in valleys,
In hidden recesses, there grow
The plants, trees, and herbs;
Trees, both great and small,
The shoots of the ripening grain,
Grape vine and sugar-cane.
Fertilized are these by the rain
And abundantly enriched;
The dry ground is soaked,
Herbs and trees flourish together.
From the one water which
Issued from that cloud,
Plants, trees, thickets, forests,
According to need receive moisture.
All the various trees,
Lofty, medium, low,
Each according to its size,
Grows and develops
Roots, stalks, branches, leaves,
Blossoms and fruits in their brilliant colours;
Wherever the one rain reaches,
All become fresh and glossy.
According as their bodies, forms
And natures are great or small,
So the enriching (rain),
Though it is one and the same,
Yet makes each of them flourish.

In like manner also the Buddha
Appears here in the World,
Like unto a great cloud
Universally covering all things;
And having appeared in the world,
He, for the sake of the living,
Discriminates and proclaims
The truth in regard to all laws.
The Great Holy World-honoured One,
Among the gods and men
And among the other beings,
Proclaims abroad this word:
'I am the Tathagata,
The Most Honoured among men;
I appear in the world
Like unto this great cloud,
To pour enrichment on all
Parched living beings,
To free them from their misery
To attain the joy of peace,
Joy of the present world,
And joy of Nirvana.
Gods, men, and every one!
Hearken well with your mind,
Come you here to me,
Behold the Peerless Honoured One!
I am the World-honoured,
Who cannot be equalled.
To give rest to every creature,
I appear in the world,
And, to the hosts of the living,

Preach the pure Law, sweet as dew;
The one and only Law
Of deliverance and Nirvana.
With one transcendent voice
I proclaim this truth,
Ever taking the Great-Vehicle
As my subject.
Upon all I ever look
Everywhere impartially,
Without distinction of persons,
Or mind of love or hate.
I have no predilections
Nor any limitations;
Ever to all beings
I preach the Law equally;
As I preach to one person,
So I preach to all.
Ever I proclaim the Law,
Engaged in naught else;
Going, coming, sitting, standing,
Never am I weary of
Pouring it copious on the world,
Like the all-enriching rain.
On honoured and humble, high and low,
Law-keepers, and law-breakers,
Those of perfect character,
And those of imperfect,
Orthodox and heterodox,
Quick witted and dull witted,
Equally I rain the Law-rain
Unwearyingly'."

VI

Turning to the great audience, the Buddha predicts for Maha-Kaśyapa and the other three elders their future as Buddhas in worlds to come, and extends his prediction to other disciples.

Maha-Kaśyapa will be the Buddha Radiance, whose realm will be Radiant Virtue, and his kalpa Magnificent.

"His domain will be beautiful, free from dirt, shards, thorns and uncleanness; its land will be level and straight with no uneven places, neither hollows nor mounds; its ground will be lapis lazuli; it will have rows of jewel-trees, golden cords to set bounds to the ways, be strewn with precious flowers, and purity will reign everywhere." Its bodhisattvas will be innumerable. "No Mara-deeds will be there, for, though Mara and Mara's people dwell in that land, they will care for its Buddha-law."

The elder Subhuti will be the Buddha Name-and-Form, in the domain Jewel-land, with crystal for its ground; his aeon will be Jewel-kalpa.

The elder Maha-Katyayana will be the Buddha Golden Light, his domain will have crystal for ground, but his kalpa and domains are described without name.

The fourth elder Maha-Maudgalyayana will be the Buddha Sandalwood Fragrance, in the domain

Gladsome Mind, with crystal for ground, and his kalpa will be Joyful.

Each section is, as usual, done into verse, but there is nothing of outstanding interest or value. The chief feature worthy of note is, that the author makes all four of the leading disciples of Śakyamuni announce their rejection of the hinayana doctrines, in favour of mahayana teaching. They proclaim their realization, which they certainly never had in their lifetime, that the Buddha's earlier teaching was temporary, awaiting the greater revelation presented in this Sutra.

VII

THE Buddha now addresses the body of his disciples, telling them that once upon a time there was a Buddha named Universal-Surpassing-Wisdom. An immeasurable time has passed since his Nirvana, and the Buddha tries to impress on his hearers the meaning of timelessness in the following manner:

"Suppose the earth element in a Three-Thousand-Great-Thousandfold-World were by some one ground into ink, and he were to pass through a thousand realms in an eastern direction, and then let fall one drop as large as a grain of dust; again, passing through another thousand realms, once more he let fall one drop; suppose he thus proceeds until he has finished the ink made of the earth-element—what is your opinion? All these realms—is it possible for mathematicians, or their disciples, to find their end or confines so as to know their number?"

"No, World-honoured One!"

"Bhikshus! Suppose all those realms which that man has passed, where he has dropped a drop and where he has not, were ground to dust, and suppose one grain of the dust be a kalpa—the time since that Buddha became extinct till now still exceeds those numbers by innumerable, infinite, hundreds, thousands, myriads, kotis of asamkhyeya kalpas. By the power of my Buddha-wisdom, I observe that distant time as if it were only to-day."

The whole story is too long for insertion here. In brief, the Buddha, Universal-Surpassing-Wisdom, after routing the army of Mara, common to Buddha-realms, sat cross-legged, motionless in mind and body, for ten minor kalpas, but still did not attain to Perfect Enlightenment.

"Then the gods of Indra's heavens spread for that Buddha a lion-throne, a yojana high, under a bodhi-tree, so that the Buddha might on this throne attain Perfect Enlightenment. No sooner was he seated on it, than the Brahma heavenly kings rained down celestial flowers over an area of a hundred yojanas. A fragrant wind from time to time arose, sweeping away the flowers as they withered and raining fresh ones."

Other wonders are described until, at the end of ten minor kalpas, the great Buddha-law of Perfect Enlightenment is revealed. His sixteen sons, born while he was a prince before he left home to become a monk, also his father, with his hundred ministers and myriads of people, all drew near to the Throne of Enlightenment, doing homage to its occupant. They besought him to roll the Wheel of the Law and proclaim the Truth.

At the moment when this Buddha attained Perfect Enlightenment the whole universe was shaken, a light shone in regions where light had never shown before, and wherever light was known its shining was doubled in intensity.

132

The Brahma-kings astonished cry:

"In all our palaces
Ne'er has been such shining:
What may be its cause?
Let us investigate.
Has a great good god been born,
Or a Buddha appeared in the world,
That this great brilliance
Illuminates the universe?"

Thereupon the Brahma-kings of the East in five hundred myriad kotis of realms, with all their palace train, each follower bearing a great bag, full of celestial flowers, set forth to investigate the sign. They found the Buddha surrounded by vast expectant throngs, and immediately joined them, strewing their flowers before his feet till they rose high as Mount Sumeru, and each offering to him his magnificent palace. In like manner there appeared, in turn, the Brahma-kings of each of the other regions, making similar offerings. This is told in plenitude of detail, covering many pages of prose and verse. The four quarters, together with the zenith and nadir, are each portrayed in similar style, with sufficient variation to avoid mere verbal repetition.

The light that shone through all the worlds was the Light of Truth dawning on the awakening Buddha. It was the Radiance of Perfect Enlightenment, of which the Mahayana is the conveyer The Brahma-kings chant:

"Kalpas untold from of yore
Have passed empty without a Buddha;
A World-honoured One not appearing,
Darkness has everywhere reigned;
The three evil states were thriving,
Flourishing were the demons,
While the heavenly host dwindled
And perished in evil estate,
Not hearing the Law from a Buddha.

. . . . .

The Buddha, the eye of the world,
Now after long ages appears;
Through pity for the living
In the world he is revealed,
Surpassing in Perfect Enlightenment

. . . . .

All our palaces, made beauteous
With this supernal Light,
We offer to the World-Honoured.

. . . . .

World-Honoured! roll the Law-wheel!
Beat the drum of the dew-sweet Law,
Save the suffering living
Reveal the Nirvana-Way!"

Then the Buddha Universal-Surpassing-Wisdom
is represented as following the tactical method of
Buddhas, that of preaching first the four noble
truths concerning Pain and its cure, i. e. the fact
and nature of suffering; the assembling (or,

focussing) of suffering; the possibility of the extinction of suffering; the way of its extinction. This he followed with the Law of the Twelve Causes of reincarnation and their annihilation. Such is, of course, the preparatory or hinayana method; yet, as the result of it, the sixteen princes and myriads of others "were freed from faults, all obtaining the profound, mystic meditations, the Three Clear (Views) and the Six Transcendent (Faculties) and thus accomplished the Eight Emancipations". Likewise, at a second, a third, and a fourth time of preaching the Law, "beings as sands of the Ganges were freed from faults."

The sixteen royal sons became monks, served myriads of Buddhas, and then besought the Buddha, their father, to preach the Law of Perfect Enlightenment! The vast host added their appeal, and "after two myriad kalpas had passed, in the midst of the four groups he preached this Mahayana Sutra named 'The Lotus Flower of the Wonderful Law'." "For eight thousand kalpas he continued preaching this Sutra without cessation. When he had finished, he then entered a quiet room and remained in meditation during eighty-four thousand kalpas." During this period his sixteen sons preached everywhere the Sutra of the Wonderful Law-Flower, saving incalculable numbers of beings.

After eighty-four thousand kalpas had passed, the Buddha, Great Universal Master of Wisdom, arose from his trance-like meditation, ascended the Law-throne, and addressed the vast assembly, calling on them to pay homage to his sixteen sons because they had universally preached the Lotus Sutra.

.   .   .   .   .

Śakyamuni, having told this story of the former Buddha, now declared that the sixteen sons, who became Buddhas, possessed their Buddha-realms in the eight directions. Two of them were in the eastern region, two in the south-eastern, and so on. Their titles are given. The fifteenth and sixteenth were in the north-eastern region, one of them being named "Destroyer of Fear in all the world", the other was Śakyamuni himself, who has now at last reached the stage of Perfect Enlightenment in this world.

He tells the disciples, that they have all been his disciples in former states of existence. "All those beings, innumerable as the sands of Ganges, whom I converted at that time, are you yourselves, and you will be my disciples in future worlds after my extinction." "In other realms I shall still be Buddha though under different names." The meaning seems to be that the One Buddha appears in countless worlds, One yet infinite in number. Each personal incarnation of the Buddhas, each embodiment, so to speak, has its own characteristic, but there is only One Buddha in and through all these various manifestations. It is, of course, not clear from this chapter alone that the One Buddha is personal, and not an abstraction like Wisdom, but the general interpretation favours one personal

6. Buddha tells his disciples the story of a former Buddha

Buddha, whom Dr. Timothy Richard has not hesitated to call God.

"Monks!" says the Buddha, "If a Tathagata himself knows that the time of his Nirvana has arrived, and that his assembly is purified, is firm in faith and discernment, penetrated with the Law of the Void, and profound in meditation, then he gathers together his bodhisattvas to preach this Sutra to them. In the world there is no second vehicle for attaining to extinction; there is only the One Buddha-Vehicle for such attainment. Know, bhikshus! The tact of the Tathagata penetrates deeply into the natures of all living beings, and knows that they are bent on the enjoyment of trifling things and deeply attached to human desires. It is for the sake of these he preaches Nirvana."

The Magic City

"Suppose, there is a fearful region, five hundred yojanas in extent, through which lies a perilous and difficult road, far from the abodes of men. Suppose there is a large company wishing to pass along that road to the Place of Jewels, and they have a guide, wise and astute, who knows well the perilous road, where it is open and where closed, and who leads the company that wish to cross this arduous region. Suppose on the way the company he leads become weary and lagging and say to the leader: 'We are utterly exhausted, and moreover afraid, and cannot go any farther; the road before us stretches far; let us turn back.' The leader, a man of much tact, reflects thus:

'These people are to be pitied. How can they give up such great treasure and seek to turn back?' Reflecting thus, by a device, in the midst of the perilous road, he magically raises a city over three hundred yojanas in extent, and says to the company: 'Do not fear, and do not turn back. Here is this great city in which you may stay and follow your own desires. If you enter this city, you will speedily be at ease; and if you then are able to go forward to the Place of Jewels, you may proceed.'

"Thereupon the exhausted company are greatly rejoiced in mind, and praise their unexampled fortune: 'Now indeed we shall escape this evil way and speedily be at ease.' Then the company proceed into the magic city, imagining they have arrived at their destination and are settled in comfort. When the leader perceives that the company are rested and are no longer fatigued, he makes the magic city disappear, and says to the company: 'Come along, all of you, the Place of Jewels is at hand. I only created this past large city for you to rest a while.'

"Bhikshus! So is it with the Tathagata. At present he is your great Leader, acquainted with the distresses, the evils, the perils and the long-continued processes of mortality, from which you must be rid and removed. If living beings only hear of One Buddha-Vehicle, they will not desire to see the Buddha, nor wish to draw nigh to him, but think thus—'the Buddha-Way is long and far; only after undergoing long and bitter toil, can the end be reached'. The Buddha, knowing how feeble and low

138

are their minds, by his tact, while they are on the way, preaches the two stages of Nirvana, in order to give them rest. If those beings remain in these secondary stages, then the Tathagata proceeds to tell them: 'You have not yet accomplished your task. The place where you are dwelling is near to the Buddha-Wisdom. Take note and ponder that the Nirvana to which you have attained is not the real one!' It is only the Tathagata's device which distinguishes and speaks of the One Buddha-Vehicle as Three. He is just like that leader who, in order to give rest to his company, magically makes a great city and after they are rested informs them saying: 'The Place of Jewels is near at hand; this city is not real, but only my magic production'."

The verse section of the Magic City is as follows:

"It is like to a perilous way,
　　Cut off, full of venomous beasts,
　　Without either water or grass,
　　A region of terror to men.
　　A throng, countless thousands, myriads,
　　Wish to traverse this perilous way,
　　Far and long indeed is the road,
　　Through five hundred yojanas.
　　Then there appears a leader,
　　Strong of sense and wise,
　　Clear-headed, resolute,
　　Who in peril saves from danger.
　　Exhausted and worn, these people
　　Cry to the leader, saying:
　　'Weary and worn are we,

Let us turn back from here.'
The leader reflects within:
'To be pitied are these poor folk!
How can they wish to turn back
And miss so great a treasure?'
Instant a device occurs—
'Let me use supernatural power
And make a great magic city,
With houses splendid adorned,
Surrounded with gardens and groves
Streamlets and bathing pools,
Massive gates and towers,
Full both of men and women.'
Making this transformation,
He pacifies them, saying: 'Fear not!
Enter all of you into this city,
Let each enjoy himself at will.'
When those people had entered the city,
Their hearts were full of joy,
They only thought of rest and ease,
And considered they had been saved.
When the leader knew they were rested,
He assembled and spoke to them saying:
'All of you now press forward!
This was but an illusory city.
Seeing you were worn out
And wishing to turn back midway,
I, therefore, by a device,
Temporarily made this city.
Do you diligently now advance
Together to the Place of Jewels.'

I, too, in equal manner,
Am the Leader of all the living.
Seeing the seekers of the Way,
Midway becoming wearied,
Unable to cross the perilous ways
Of mortality and delusion.
So I, by expedient methods,
For their ease preached Nirvana, saying:
'Your sufferings now are ended;
All your toil is finished!'
When I knew you had reached Nirvana
And all had become Arhats,
Then I gathered you together
And preached to you the real Law.
Buddhas in their tactfulness,
Separately preach the Three Vehicles;
Though there is but the One Buddha-Vehicle;
Only as resting-places are Two preached.
Now I preach to you the truth;
What you have reached is not the extinction.
To obtain perfect Buddha-knowledge,
Exert yourselves with utmost zeal!
Prove the Perfect Knowledge,
The Ten Powers of the Buddha-Laws,
Perfect the Thirty-two Signs—
Then that is the real extinction.
The Buddhas, the onward Leaders,
Call the resting-place Nirvana,
But, perceiving their people rested,
They lead on to Buddha-Wisdom."

VIII

Leaving his seat, the disciple Purna now prostrates himself before the Buddha, then rises and gazes transfixed upon his honoured countenance. Thereupon the Buddha praises Purna as the greatest of his preachers, not only in this world, but in many previous existences under many Buddhas. He foretells that when he has accomplished his course he will become the Buddha Radiance-of-the-Law, whose land will consist of "the seven precious things", "its ground level as the palm of the hand, free from hills and valleys, runnels and ditches". In its sky, "men and gods will meet and behold each other. There will be no evil ways, and no womankind, for all living beings will be born by transformation and have no carnal passion. They will attain to great transcendent powers; their bodies will emit rays of light; they will fly anywhere at will". Their food will be Joy-in-the-Law, and Gladness-in-Meditation. His domain will be Excellent-Purity and his kalpa Jewel-Radiance.

In the verse section occur the following lines:
"Bhikshus! Attentively listen to me!
The Way my Buddha-son has walked,
Through studying well expediency,
Surpasses all conception far.
Knowing all beings enjoy mere trifles

And are afraid of the greater wisdom,
The Bodhisattvas, therefore, become
Sravakas or Pratyekabuddhas.
By numberless expedient methods
All kinds of beings they then convert,
Saying: 'We are only Sravakas,
Far removed from Buddhahood.'
Innumerable beings they thus release,
Each completing his varied course;
Even the lax and low-disposed
Become Buddhas by gradual stage.
Hiding their Bodhisattva-deeds,
Externally they are as Sravakas;
With few desires, disliking mortal life,
They truly purify their Buddha-land,
Appearing possessed of human passions
And seeming to hold heretical views.
Thus do my disciples
Tactfully save all beings.
If I fully explained
Their varied transformations,
Beings who heard of them
Would be perplexed and puzzled.

.   .   .   .

Their meat is joy in the Law
And pleasure in meditation,
With never a thought of other;
No womankind will be there,
Nor any evil ways.
My disciple Bhikshu Purna,

His merits all complete,
Shall gain this pure land
Where the wise and the sage abound.
Such are the measureless things
I have now but briefly hinted."

After this the Buddha predicts the future of five hundred other disciples, each of whom, when he has served sixty-two thousand kotis of Buddhas, will themselves, one after another, become Buddhas, each of whom will be called Universal-Light. These five hundred disciples,

"ecstatic with joy, instantly rise from their seats, go before the Buddha, make obeisance at his feet, repent of their errors, and rebuke themselves, saying: 'World-honoured One! We have constantly been thinking we had attained to final Nirvana. Now we know that we were just as the foolish ones. Wherefore? Because we ought to have obtained the Tathagata-wisdom, and yet were content with the inferior knowledge.

"World-honoured One! It is as if some man goes to an intimate friend's house, gets drunk, and falls asleep. Meanwhile his friend, having to go forth on official duty, ties a priceless jewel within the man's garment as a present, and departs. The man being drunk and asleep knows nothing of this. On arising he travels onwards till he reaches some other country where, striving for food and clothing, he labours diligently, undergoes exceeding great hardship, and is content even if he can obtain but a little. Later, his friend happens to meet him and speaks thus—'Tut!

Sir! How is it you have come down to this, merely for the sake of food and clothing? Wishing you to be in comfort and able to satisfy your five senses, I formerly in such a year and month and on such a day, tied a priceless jewel within your garment. Now as of old it is present there, yet you in ignorance are slaving and worrying to keep yourself alive. How very stupid! Go you now and exchange that jewel for what you need, and for ever hereafter live as you will, free from poverty and shortage.' "

"Like this also were we.
For long has the One World-honoured
Always pitied and taught us
To cultivate supreme aspiration;
But, because of our ignorance,
We neither perceived nor knew it;
Gaining but a trifle of Nirvana,
Contented we sought no more.
Now the Buddha awakens us,
Saying this is not real Nirvana;
In attaining supreme Buddha-wisdom,
Does real Nirvana lie.
Now we, having heard from the Buddha
Our prediction and its glory,
And the command we receive in turn,
Full of joy are we, body and soul."

IX

THE beloved disciple of Śakyamuni was Ananda,
sometimes spoken of as the St. John of the Buddha.
He it was whose memory guarded the Treasury,
or Doctrine of the Master's Law. Rahula was
Śakyamuni's son born while he was Prince
Gautama. These two, Ananda and Rahula now
come forward to the feet of Buddha. Both prostrate themselves and implore that they too may
share in this Mahayana glory.

"Ananda is always thy attendant, protecting and
keeping the treasury of the Law, and Rahula is the
Buddha's son. If the Buddha sees fit to predict us to
Perfect Enlightenment, our desires will be fulfilled
and every hope be satisfied."

"Thereupon two thousand disciples, who had completed their hinayana training, all rose from their
seats, bared their right shoulders, went before the
Buddha, with one mind folded their hands, and gazed
upon the World-honoured One, wishing as Ananda
and Rahula wished, and stood there in line.

"Then the Buddha speaking to Ananda said: 'In
a future world you will become a Buddha with the
title of Sovereign-Universal-King-of-Wisdom Moun-
tain-high and Ocean-deep'." His domain would be
"Never-lowered Banner of Victory", and his aeon
"Full of Wonder-Sound."

Then follows this arresting endeavour to depict
infinity:

"His lifetime will be such immeasurable thousands,
myriads, kotis of numberless kalpas, that even if a

man tried to count them through thousands, myriads, kotis, immeasurable, numberless kalpas it would be impossible to know it."

A certain perplexity and seeming envy is bruited among eight thousand bodhisattvas in the assembly, which the Buddha appeases by explaining the favour done to Ananda in this prediction. He tells them that he and Ananda first met in the realm of the Buddha King-of-the-Firmament, and there they together attained the concept of Perfect Enlightenment. Ananda was the more meditative; Sakyamuni the more energetic. Consequently Sakyamuni first attained to Buddhahood, while Ananda became the studious rememberer of his teaching. Until Ananda becomes Buddha, therefore, he will continue to be Guardian-of-the-Law of future Buddhas, and instruct and bring to perfection the host of bodhisattvas. "Such was his original vow, and consequently he receives this prediction."

Instantly Ananda recalls to mind the Law-treasuries in the past of unlimited myriads, kotis of Buddhas, and understands them without difficulty as if he were now hearing them, recalling also his original vow:

> "The rare World-honoured One
> Recalls to my mind the Law
> Of countless Buddhas past,
> As if I were hearing it to-day.
> I now, having no more doubts,

Take up my abode in Buddhahood.
With skilfulness will I serve
And care for the Buddha's Law."

Of Rahula it is foretold that he will become a Buddha entitled "Treader on Seven-jewelled Lotuses". He will "pay homage to Buddha-Tathagatas equal in number to the atoms of ten worlds, always as the eldest son of those Buddhas, just as at present". The Buddha says:

"When I was prince-royal
Rahula was my eldest son.
Now that I have attained Buddhahood
He, as Law-heir, inherits the Law.
In ages of the future,
Seeing infinite kotis of Buddhas,
To all he will be eldest son,
Whole-hearted seeking Buddhahood."

The two thousand who, with appealing looks stand expectant, are now blessed in like manner. They will each attain to be Buddhas, at the same time obtaining a realm in infinite space. The title of each Buddha will be "Jewel Emblem" and their realms in every respect will be equal.

"In the future they will every one be Buddhas.

.   .   .   .   .   .

And will reach Perfect Enlightenment.
In domains in all directions
Each will have the same title.
Simultaneously on wisdom-thrones
They will prove the Supreme Wisdom."

X

THE Great Bodhisattva, mythical King of Healing, is now called forth by the Buddha. Through him he addresses the "eighty thousand great leaders", saying:

"King of Healing! Do you see in this assembly innumerable gods, dragon-kings, yakshas, gandharvas, asuras, garudas, kinnaras, mahoragas, human and non-human beings, as well as monks, nuns, male and female lay devotees, seekers after bodhisattvahood, sravakahood, seekers after pratyeka-buddhahood, and seekers after Buddhahood? Such beings as these, in the presence of the Buddha, if they hear but a single verse, or a single word of the Wonderful Law-Flower Sutra, and even by a single thought delight in it, I predict they will attain to Perfect Enlightenment."

"Again, let there be any who receive, keep, read, recite, expound or copy even a single verse of the Wonderful Law-Flower Sutra, and look upon this Sutra with reverence as if it were the Buddha, and make offerings to it in various ways with flowers, perfume, garlands, sandal-powder, perfumed unguents, incense for burning, silk-canopies, banners, flags, garments, and music, or even pay homage to it with folded hands; know, King of Healing, it is a sign that these people have already paid homage to ten myriad kotis of Buddhas, and under the Buddhas performed their great vows; therefore out of compassion for all living beings, they are born among men.

"King of Healing! If there be any people who ask you what sort of living beings will become Buddhas in future worlds, you should show them that these are the people who will certainly become Buddhas in those worlds. Wherefore? If my good sons and good daughters receive and keep, read and recite, or expound, and copy even a single word in the Law-Flower Sutra, and make offerings to it in various ways with flowers, perfumes, garlands, sandal-powder, fragrant unguents, incense for burning, silk-canopies, banners, flags, garments, and music, and revere it with folded hands, these people should be looked up to by all the worlds; and just as you pay homage to Tathagatas, so should you pay homage to them. Know! These people are great Bodhisattvas who, having accomplished Perfect Enlightenment and out of compassion for all living beings, are willingly born into this world, widely to proclaim and expound the Wonderful Law-Flower Sutra. How much more those who are perfectly able to receive, keep, and in every way pay homage to it! Know, King of Healing! These people will of themselves abandon the reward of their purified karma, and after my extinction, out of pity for all living beings, will be re-born in the evil world and widely proclaim this Sutra. If these good sons and daughters, after my extinction, should be able, even by stealth, to preach to one person but one word of the Law-Flower Sutra, know, these people are Tathagata-messengers sent by the Tathagata, to perform Tathagata-deeds. How much more so those who in great assemblies widely preach it to others!

"King of Healing! Even if there be some wicked person who out of an evil mind, throughout a whole kalpa, in presence of the Buddha, unceasingly abuses the Buddha, his sin is still light. But if any one, even with a single ill word, defames lay devotees or monks who read and recite the Law-Flower Sutra, his sin is extremely heavy. King of Healing! Know that he who reads and recites the Law-Flower Sutra—that man has adorned himself with the adornment of Buddha, and so is carried by the Tathagata on his shoulder. Wherever he goes, he should be saluted with hands whole-heartedly folded, revered, worshipped, honoured, and extolled, and offerings made to him of flowers, perfumes, garlands, sandal-powder, perfumed unguents, incense for burning, silk-canopies, banners, flags, garments, edibles and dainties, and music—he should be served with the most excellent offerings found amongst men. Celestial jewels should be scattered before him and heaped offerings made of celestial jewels. Wherefore? Because this man delighting to preach the Law, they who hear it but for a moment thereupon attain to Perfect Enlightenment."

Then the World-honoured One, desiring to proclaim this teaching over again, spoke thus in verse:

"Should one wish to dwell in Buddhahood
And attain to intuitive Wisdom,
He must always earnestly honour

The keepers of the Flower of the Law.
Should one wish quickly to attain
To complete omniscience,
He must receive and keep this Sutra
And honour those who keep it.
Should one be able to receive and keep
The Wonderful Law-Flower Sutra,
Let him know he is the Buddha's messenger,
Who compassionates all living beings.
He who is able to receive and keep
The Wonderful Law-Flower Sutra,
Casting aside his Paradise, and,
From pity for the living, being re-born,
Know, such a man as this,
Free to be born where he will,
Is able, in this evil world,
Widely to preach the Supreme Law.
You should, with celestial flowers and perfumes,
Robes of heavenly jewels, and heaps
Of wonderful celestial jewels,
Pay homage to such a preacher of the Law.
In evil ages after my extinction
Those who are able to keep this Sutra
Must be worshipped with folded hands,
As if paying homage to the World-honoured One.
With the best of dainties and sweets,
And every kind of garment,
This son of Buddha should be worshipped
In hope of hearing him if but for a moment.
In future ages, if one is able
To receive and keep this Sutra,

I will send him to be amongst men,
To perform the task of the Tathagata."

Again he addresses the King of Healing:

"Infinite thousands, myriads of kotis are the Sutras
I preach, whether already preached, now being
preached, or to be preached in the future. Among
them all this Law-Flower Sutra is the most difficult
to believe and the most difficult to apprehend. King
of Healing! This Sutra is the very treasury of the
secret of the Buddhas, and may not be recklessly
offered to men. It is guarded by Buddhas, World-
honoured Ones, and from of yore has never been
divulged in the world. This Sutra, even while the
Buddha is still here, has aroused much enmity and
envy; how much more after his Nirvana?"

Thus does the author indicate that the doctrine of
The Lotus is new and subversive. The fact that he
puts the new doctrine into the lips of a spiritualized
Buddha, in the form of a religious drama or apocalypse, is far from patent to his Mahayana followers
who, as already stated, believe it to have been Sakyamuni's final doctrine while here on this earth.

"Know, King of Healing! After the Tathagata enters
Nirvana, those who are able to copy, keep, read,
recite, worship or preach it to others, will be invested
by the Tathagata with his robes, and will be protected
and remembered by Buddhas now abiding in other
regions. . . . Know, these people shall dwell with
the Tathagata, and his hand shall be upon their
heads.

153

"King of Healing! In every place where this Sutra is preached, or read, or recited, or copied, or its volumes kept, one should erect a Stupa of the Precious Seven, making it very high, spacious and splendid. But there is no need to deposit any relics. Wherefore? Because in it there is the whole body of the Tathagata (i.e. this Sutra). This Sutra should be served, revered, honoured, and extolled with all kinds of flowers, perfumes, garlands, silk-canopies, banners, flags, music, and hymns. If any, seeing that Stupa, salute and worship it, know, that they all are near to Perfect Enlightenment. King of Healing! Many people there are, both laymen and monks, who walk in the Bodhisattva-Way, without, as it were, being able to see, hear, read, recite, copy, keep, and worship this Law-Flower Sutra. Know, that those people are not yet rightly walking in the Bodhisattva-Way. But if any hear this Sutra, then they shall be able to walk aright in the Bodhisattva-Way. If any living beings who seek after the Buddha-Way, either see or hear this Law-Flower Sutra, and after hearing it believe and discern, receive and keep it, you may know that they are near to Perfect Enlightenment.

"This Sutra opens the way from the expedient, partial method to the full revelation of truth and reality. The treasury of this Law-Flower Sutra is so deep and secure, so hidden and remote that no human being can reach it. But now the Buddha has revealed it for instructing bodhisattvas and bringing them to perfection."

Should any good son or daughter resolve to preach

154

this Sutra, let that good son or daughter "enter into the Dwelling of the Tathagata, be clad with the Robe of the Tathagata, and sit on the Seat of the Tathagata. . . . The Dwelling of the Tathagata is the great compassionate heart within all the living. The Robe of the Tathagata is the gentle and forbearing heart. The Seat of the Tathagata is the "Spirituality of all Existence".

"King of Healing! I, though dwelling in another realm, will send spirit-messengers to gather together hearers of the Law for that preacher, and also send spirit monks and nuns, male and female devotees, to hear such a one preach the Law. All these spirit-people, hearing this Law, will unresistingly receive it in faith and obey it. If the preacher of this Law should abide in a place remote from the world, I will abundantly send gods, dragons, spirits, and others to listen. Though I am in a different domain, I will from time to time cause the preachers of this Law to behold me. If such a one forgets any detail of this Sutra, I will return and tell him, that he may be in perfect possession of it.

"If, when he preaches this Sutra,
Some with ill mouth should abuse,
Lay on swords, sticks, shards or stones,
Let him think of the Buddha and be patient.
In thousands, myriads of lands
I will appear with unperishing body
And, in infinite kotis of kalpas,
Preach this Law for all the living.

. . . . .

155

Dwells he alone in secluded place,
In solitude with no voice of man,
. . . .
Then I unto him will appear
With a pure and shining body."

XI

ON to the stage now comes perhaps the most dramatic scene in the whole pageant. Suddenly there springs up from the earth, to the midst of the sky, a Stupa or Shrine, of stupendous size and magnificence. It is made of the seven precious things, that is, gold, silver, and various precious stones. It is

"splendidly adorned with five thousand parapets, thousands, myriads of recesses, and countless banners and flags; it is hung with jewel garlands; myriads and kotis of gem-bells are suspended on it. From it comes the exquisite fragrance of rare sandal-wood, filling the whole world. The thirty-three celestial gods rain celestial flowers upon it. The vast assembly of beings, gods, human and non-human beings pay homage to it."

From the midst of the Shrine there comes a mighty voice saying:

"Excellent! Excellent! World-honoured Sakyamuni! Thou art able to preach to the great assembly the Wonderful Law-Flower Sutra of universal and mighty Wisdom, by which bodhisattvas are instructed and which the Buddhas themselves guard and teach. Thus it is, thus it is, World-honoured Sakyamuni! All is true that thou sayest."

The Spirit-Bodhisattva "Great Eloquence" asks on behalf of the assembly:

"For what reason has this Stupa sprung out of the earth and from its midst this voice proceeded?"

Then Śākyamuni Buddha replies:

"In this Stupa is the whole body of the Tathāgata. Of yore, in the past, innumerable thousands, myriads, kotis of asamkhyeya worlds away in the east, there was a domain named 'Jewel-clear'. In that domain there was a Buddha named 'Abundant Treasures'. When that Buddha was treading the Bodhisattva-Way, he made a great vow, saying: 'After I become a Buddha and am extinct, if in any country in the universe there be a place where the Law-Flower Sutra is preached, let my Stupa arise and appear there, in order that I may hearken to that Sutra, bear testimony to it and extol it, saying "Excellent".' When that Buddha had finished his course and his extinction was approaching, in the midst of gods, men, and a great host, he instructed his bhikshus: 'After my extinction, those who desire to worship my whole body should erect a great Stupa.' Wherever in the worlds of the universe, the Law-Flower Sutra is preached, that Buddha, by the supernatural powers of his vow, causes his Stupa containing his whole body to spring forth and praises the Sutra saying, 'Excellent! Excellent!' Great Eloquence! It is because just now the Tathāgata 'Abundant Treasures' heard the Law-Flower Sutra being preached, that his Stupa sprang up from the earth and he extolled the Sutra saying 'Excellent! Excellent!'"

"Thereupon the Bodhisattva Great-Eloquence, because of the divine power of the Tathāgata, said to

7. The light from the Buddha's brow announcing to all the worlds that he is about to preach the Lotus Sutra, and the sudden appearance of the Ancient Buddha in his shrine

the Buddha: 'World-honoured One! We earnestly desire to see this Buddha.'

"The Buddha then addressed the Bodhisattva-Mahasattva Great-Eloquence thus: 'This Buddha, Abundant-Treasures, has a profound and grave vow: "When my Stupa appears in the presence of any Buddha that I may hear the Law-Flower Sutra, if he desires to show me to his four groups, let the Buddhas who have emanated from that Buddha, and who are preaching the Law in the worlds in all directions, together return and assemble in one place, and then will I appear in person". So, Great-Eloquence, I must now assemble the Buddhas who have emanated from me and who are preaching the Law in the worlds in every direction.'

"Great-Eloquence replied to the Buddha: 'World-honoured One! We would also see the Buddhas emanated from the World-honoured One and worship and pay homage to them.'

"Then the Buddha sent forth a ray from the white curl between his eyebrows, whereupon eastward there became visible the Buddhas in five hundred myriad kotis of nayutas of domains, as the sands of Ganges. All those domains had crystal for earth, jewel-trees and precious textures for adornment, were filled with countless thousands, myriads, kotis of Bodhisattvas, with jewelled canopies stretched above them, covered with network of jewels. All the Buddhas in those domains were preaching the laws with ravishing voices, and innumerable thousands, myriads, kotis of Bodhisattvas were also seen, filling

159

those domains and preaching to the multitudes. So, too, was it in the southern, western, and northern quarters, in the four intermediate directions, in the zenith, and the nadir, wherever shone the ray-signal from the white curl.

"Then the Buddhas in every direction each addressed the host of his Bodhisattvas saying: 'Good sons! We must now go to Śakyamuni Buddha in the Saha-world, and pay homage to the Precious Stupa of the Tathagata 'Abundant-Treasures'.

"Thereupon this Saha-world instantly became pure, with lapis lazuli for earth, adorned with jewel-trees, cords made of gold marking the boundaries of its eight divisions; having no hamlets, villages, towns, cities, great seas, great rivers, mountains, streams, forests, and thickets; smoking with most precious incense; its ground strewn with mandarva-flowers, spread with precious nets and curtains, and hung with all kinds of precious bells.

"There remained only the assembled congregation, all other gods and men having been removed to other lands. Then those Buddhas, each bringing a great Bodhisattva as his attendant, arrived at the Saha-world and each went to the foot of a jewel-tree. Every jewel-tree was five hundred yojanas high, adorned in turn with boughs, leaves, blossoms, and fruit; under those jewel-trees there were lion-thrones, five yojanas high, also decorated with magnificent jewels. Then each of those Buddhas sat cross-legged on his throne.

"Thus all around him the Three-Thousand-Great-

Thousandfold World was filled with Buddhas; though as yet, from even one point of the compass, the Buddhas who had emanated from Śakyamuni Buddha had not finished arriving. Then Śakyamuni Buddha, desiring to make room for the Buddhas who had emanated from himself, in each of the eight directions of space transformed two hundred myriad kotis of nayutas of domains, all of them pure, without hells, hungry spirits, animals, and asuras, and also removed their gods and men to other lands. The domains thus transformed also had lapis lazuli for earth and were ornate with jewel-trees, five hundred yojanas high, adorned in turn with boughs, leaves, blossoms, and fruits; under every tree was a jewelled lion-throne, five yojanas high, decorated with every kind of gem; and there were no great seas, nor great rivers, nor any mountains."

More and more vast worlds were transformed in like manner to receive the approaching throng.

"At that moment the Buddha-bodies which had emanated eastward from Śakyamuni, namely, the Buddhas who were each preaching the Law in hundreds, thousands, myriads, kotis of nayutas of eastern domains as the sands of Ganges, arrived and assembled. In like manner in turn the Buddhas from the ten directions all arrived and assembled and took their seats in the eight directions. Thereupon each direction was filled with Buddha-Tathagatas from its four hundred myriad kotis of nayutas of domains. Then the Buddhas, each under a jewel-tree, seated on a lion-throne, sent their attendants to make inquiries of Śakyamuni Buddha, each sending a double handful of jewel-flowers.

"Then Śakyamuni Buddha, beholding the Buddhas who had emanated from him assembled together, each seated on his lion-throne, and hearing that those Buddhas unitedly desired the Precious Stupa to be opened, straightway rose up from his throne, and took his place in the Sky. The four groups stood up, folded their hands, and with all their mind gazed at the Buddha. Thereupon Śakyamuni Buddha with his right fingers opened the door of the Stupa of the Precious Seven, when there went forth a great sound, like the withdrawing of the bolt on opening a great city gate. Thereupon all the congregation saw the Tathagata 'Abundant Treasures' sitting on the lion-throne in the Precious Stupa, with his undissipated body whole and as if he were in meditation. And they heard him say: 'Excellent! Excellent! Śakyamuni Buddha! Speedily preach the Law-Flower Sutra. I have come hither in order to hear this Sutra.'

"Then the four groups, seeing the Buddha who had passed away and been extinct for immeasurable thousands, myriads, kotis of kalpas, speak such words as these, praised the unprecedented marvel, and strewed on the Buddha 'Abundant Treasures' and on Śakyamuni Buddha heaps of celestial jewel-flowers. Thereupon the Buddha 'Abundant Treasures' within the Precious Stupa shared half his throne with Śakyamuni Buddha, speaking thus: 'Śakyamuni

Buddha! Take this seat!' Whereupon Śakyamuni Buddha entered into the Stupa and sitting down on that half throne folded his legs. Then the great assembly, seeing the two Tathagatas sitting cross-legged on the lion-throne in the Stupa of the Precious Seven, reflected thus: 'The Buddhas are sitting aloft and far away. Would that the Tathagatas, by their transcendent power, might cause us together to take up our abode in the Sky!' Immediately Śakya-muni Buddha, by his transcendent power, received all the great assembly up into the Sky, and with a great voice, universally addressed the four groups saying: 'Who is able to declare the Wonderful Law-Flower Sutra in this Saha-world? Now indeed is the time. The Tathagata not long hence must enter Nirvana. The Buddha desires to bequeath this Wonderful Law-Flower Sutra, so that it may ever exist'."

The dramatic and apocalyptic character of the work is no more clearly evident than in this chapter. The splendid imagery of the ancient Buddha appearing in his shrine, poised in the sky, the unbolting of the door, the invitation to Śakyamuni to sit by him, the still more striking conception of raising the whole congregation into the heavens, even from a world already purified and expanded, in which no longer was there any mountain, nor sea, nor river—all this presentation of a gorgeous vision, such as no earthly eyes could see, exhibits a Buddhism never preached by Śakyamuni while on earth. Had the Mahayanists declared this Sutra to be a revelation made by Śakyamuni after his withdrawal from earth, their position would have been less vulnerable.

The verse section has passages such as the following, the speaker being Śakyamuni:

"The Holy World-honoured Lord,
Albeit for long extinct,
And in his Precious Stupa,
Yet comes to hear the Law.
How then can any not be
Zealous in the Law?
  This Buddha has been extinct
For countless numbers of kalpas.
Yet from place to place he goes,
To hear this rarely-preached Law.
This Buddha of old made a vow—
'After my final extinction,
I will wander anywhere
And ever to hear this Law.'
  Innumerable Buddhas,
Who emanated from my person,
Many as sands of Ganges,
Have come to hear the Law,
And to behold the long extinct
Tathagata 'Abundant Treasures'.
Each, leaving his wonderful land
And his multitude of disciples,
Gods, men, and nagas,
And all their offerings,
Has come here to this place
To ensure the Law will long abide.
  In order to seat these Buddhas,

164

By my transcendent powers,
I have removed innumerable beings
And cleared my own domain."

Again:

"Whoever is able to care
For the Law of this Sutra
Will be deemed to have worshipped
Me and 'Abundant Treasures',
This Buddha 'Abundant Treasures',
Who dwells in the Precious Stupa,
And wanders everywhere
For the sake of this Sutra.
He will moreover have worshipped
These my emanated Buddhas,
Who adorn and make resplendent
All worlds everywhere.
If he preaches this Sutra,
Then he is deemed to have seen me
And the Tathagata 'Abundant Treasures',
Also my emanated Buddhas.
    All ye, my good sons!
Let each carefully ponder
That this is a difficult task,
Needing a great vow.
All the other sutras,
Numerous as sands of Ganges,
Though one expounded them all,
'Twould still not be counted hard.
If one took up Sumeru
And hurled it to another region

Over numerous Buddha-lands,
Neither would that be hard.
If one were with his toes
To move a Great Chiliocosm
And hurl it afar to another land,
That also would not be hard.
If one stood on the summit of All things,
And expounded to all beings
The countless other sutras,
That also would not be hard.
But if, after the Buddha's extinction,
In the midst of an evil world,
One is able to preach this Sutra,
This indeed is hard.

Though there should be a man
Who grasps the sky in his hand
And with it wanders about,
That is still not hard.
But if, after my extinction,
One himself should copy and keep,
Or cause another to copy this Sutra,
That indeed is hard.

If one took the great earth,
Put it on his toe-nail
And ascended to the Brahma-heaven,
That would still not be hard.
But, after the Buddha's extinction,
In the midst of an evil world,
To read aloud this Sutra for a moment,
That indeed will be hard.

Though one, in the last conflagration,

Should carry a load of dry hay,
And pass through the fire unseared,
That would still not be hard.
But, after my extinction,
If any one keeps this Sutra
And proclaims it to one man only,
That indeed will be hard.
   If one kept the Eighty-four Thousand
Sections of the Law
And the Twelve Divisions of Sutras,
Expounded them also to others,
And caused those who heard to gain
The Six Transcendent Powers—
Though he had such power as this,
That would still not be hard.
But if, after my extinction,
One hears and receives this Sutra
And searches into its meaning,
That indeed will be hard."

Again:

   "I, on account of Buddhahood,
In innumerable lands
From the beginning until now,
Have expounded many Sutras;
But, amongst them all,
This Sutra is the chief,
If any one is able to keep it,
Then he keeps the Buddha's Body.
   All you, my good sons!
Let him who, on my extinction,

Is able to receive and keep,
Read and recite this Sutra,
Now in presence of the Buddha,
Himself announce his vow!
This Sutra so hard to keep,
If one keeps it but a short time,
I shall still be pleased,
And so will all the Buddhas.
    Such a one as this
Will be praised by all the Buddhas;
Such a one is brave;
Such a one is zealous;
Such a one is named Law-keeper
And Dhuta-observer;
Speedily shall he attain
To Supreme Buddhahood.
He who in the future
Can read and keep this Sutra,
Is truly a Buddha-son,
Dwelling in the stage of pure goodness.
After the Buddha's extinction,
He who can expound its meaning,
Will be the eye of the world
For both gods and men.
He who, in the last age of fear,
Can preach it but for a moment,
By gods and men
Will be venerated."

XII

THAT this chapter may be an interpolation is explained in the Introduction. It proceeds to recount how Śakyamuni, ages ago, "through innumerable aeons tirelessly sought the Law-Flower Sutra."

"During many kalpas I was long a king and vowed to seek the Supreme Wisdom, my mind never relenting." "I bestowed alms unstintingly—elephants, horses, the seven precious things, countries, cities, wives, children, male and female slaves, servants and followers, head, eyes,· marrow, brain, the flesh of my body, hands, and feet, unsparing of body and life. At that time people's lifetime was beyond measure. For the sake of the Law, I gave up the throne of my domain, deputed my government to the prince-royal, and with beating drum and open proclamation, sought everywhere for the truth, promising—'Whoever is able to tell me of a Great-Vehicle, him I will all my life provide for, and be his footman.' At that time a certain hermit came to me, the king, and said: 'I have a Great-Vehicle, named Wonderful Law-Flower Sutra. If you will not disobey me, I will explain it to you.' I, the king, hearing what the hermit said, became ecstatic with joy and instantly followed, providing for his needs, gathering fruit, drawing water, collecting fuel, laying his food, even of my body making his seat and bed, yet never feeling fatigue of body or mind. While I thus served a millenium passed, and for the sake of the Law, I zealously waited on him that he should lack nothing."

"The aforetime king was myself and the sage at that juncture was the present Devadatta himself."

Then he foretells the future destiny of Devadatta, that he will become a Buddha named "Deva-king", or "King of the gods".

"If there be, in a future world, any good son or good daughter who hears this Devadatta chapter of the Wonderful Law-Flower Sutra, with pure heart and believing reverence, and is free from doubt, such a one shall not fall into the hells or become a hungry spirit or animal, but shall be born into the presence of the Buddhas of the universe. Wherever he be born he will always hear this Sutra; and whether he be born amongst men or gods, he will enjoy marvellous delight. As to the Buddha into whose presence he is born, his birth shall be by transformation from a lotus-flower."

Thereupon one of the attendants on the Buddha "Abundant Treasures" within the Stupa, by name "Wisdom-Store", says to his master: "Let us return to our own land!" But Śakyamuni Buddha answers Wisdom-Store: "Good son! Wait a while. Here is the Bodhisattva, Manjuśri. First meet and discuss with him the Wonderful Law and then return to your own land."

"Thereupon Manjuśri, sitting on a thousand-petal lotus-flower, large as a carriage-wheel, and the Bodhisattvas who accompany him, also sitting on jewelled lotus-flowers, unaided spring up from the great ocean, out of the palace of the Sagara Dragon-King. Taking up his place in the sky, he advances to the Divine Vulture Peak, alights from his lotus-flower, goes before the Buddha, and reverently makes obeisance at the feet of the two World-honoured Ones. When he has expressed his reverence he goes over to Wisdom-Store and, after they have asked of each other's welfare, they withdraw and sit on one side. The Bodhisattva Wisdom-Store asks Manju-śri: 'Virtuous Sir! Since you went to the Dragon palace, how many beings have you converted?' Manju-śri answers: 'Their numbers are immeasurable, they cannot be calculated, nor expressed in words, nor fathomed by the mind. Wait but a moment: let me give the proof.' Before he has finished speaking numberless Bodhisattvas, sitting on jewelled lotus-flowers, spring up from the sea, advance to the Divine Vulture Peak, and take their places in the Sky. All these Bodhisattvas have been converted and saved by Manjuśri."

Then the Bodhisattva Wisdom-Store extols him thus in verse:

"Most wise, brave and strong one!
  Thou hast converted countless beings,
  As now this great assembly
  And I have all seen.
  Expounding the principle of Reality
  And revealing the One-Vehicle Law,
  Widely hast thou led the living
  To attain with speed to Bodhi."

171

Manjuśri replies: "That which in the midst of the ocean I always proclaimed, was no other than the Wonderful Law-Flower Sutra."

Wisdom-Store asks Manjuśri: "This Sutra is very profound and subtle, the pearl of all the Sutras, a rarity in the world. Is there any being who, diligently and zealously practising this Sutra, can attain speedily to Buddhahood?"

"There is the daughter of the Dragon-King Sagara," Manjuśri replies, "just eight years old, wise and keen of faculties, well acquainted with the karma arising from the roots of action of all creatures, who has obtained dharani, has been able to receive and keep all the most profound and mystic treasuries revealed by Buddhas, and has deeply entered into meditations and penetrated into all laws. In a moment of time, she resolved on Bodhi and attained to non-relapse to mortality. She has unembarassed powers of argument, and has a compassionate mind for all the living as if they were her children; her merits are complete and the thoughts of her mind and discourses of her mouth are both subtle and great. Kind and compassionate, virtuous and modest, gentle and beautiful in her disposition, she has been able to attain to Bodhi."

The Bodhisattva Wisdom-Store doubtingly replies: "I have seen how Sakyamuni Tathagata, during innumerable kalpas, in doing arduous and painful deeds, accumulating merit and heaping up virtue, sought the Way of Bodhi ceaselessly and without rest. I have observed that in his Three-Thousand-Great-

8. The Dragon King comes up from the ocean to receive the Buddha's instruction

Thousandfold-Worlds there is not even a spot as small as a mustard-seed where he has not laid down his body and life as a Bodhisattva, for the sake of the living; and only after that has he attained to Bodhi. It is incredible that this girl, in but a moment, should become perfectly enlightened."

"Before he has ceased talking, the daughter of the Dragon-King suddenly appears before them and, after making reverent obeisance to the Buddha, withdraws to one side, extolling Him thus in verse:

> "Profound seer of sin and goodness,
> Illuminator of the universe;
> Whose spiritual body, ethereal and pure,
> Has the Thirty-two perfect Signs;
> With the Eighty kinds of Excellence
> Is his Spiritual Body adorned;
> To whom gods and men look up,
> Nagas and spirits pay reverence,
> And all species of living beings
> Pay their worship and honour;
> Hearing the Truth, I attained to Bodhi;
> To this only a Buddha may bear witness.
> I will reveal the Great-Vehicle teaching
> Which delivers creatures from suffering."

Thereupon Śariputra says to the daughter of the Dragon-king:

"You state that in no length of time you attained to the Supreme Way. This thing is hard to believe. Wherefore? Because the body of a woman is filthy and not a vessel of the Law. How can she attain to

Supreme Bodhi? Buddhahood is so vast that only after passing through innumerable kalpas, enduring hardship, accumulating good works, and perfectly practising the Perfections, can it be accomplished. Moreover, a woman by her body still has five hindrances, viz., she cannot become, firstly, king of the Brahma-heaven: secondly, Sakra; thirdly, a Mara-king; fourthly, a Holy Wheel-rolling King; and fifthly, a Buddha. How then could a woman's body so speedily become a Buddha?"

"Now the Dragon's daughter possesses a precious pearl, worth a Three-Thousand-Great-Thousand-fold-World, which she holds up and presents to the Buddha, and which the Buddha immediately accepts. The Dragon's daughter then says to the Bodhisattva Wisdom-Store and the Honoured Śariputra:

" 'I have offered my pearl, and the World-honoured One has accepted it—was this action speedy?'

" 'Most speedy' they answered.

" 'By your supernatural powers behold me become a Buddha, even more rapidly than that!' says the daughter.

"At this moment the entire congregation sees the Dragon's daughter suddenly transformed into a male, perfect in Bodhisattva-deeds, who instantly goes to the World 'Spotless' in the southern quarter, where she sits on a precious lotus-flower, attaining perfect enlightenment, with the Thirty-two Signs and the Eighty kinds of Excellence, and universally proclaiming the Wonderful Law to every living creature in the universe."

174

Great is the rejoicing that follows among the disciples, as also amongst gods and the spirits, high and low, and many are converted or make progress in faith and powers.

The immediate conversion of the daughter of the dragon-king into a Buddha is a remarkable tribute to the spirit of the Lotus doctrine, revealing its freedom from every hindrance to the Universal Salvation it preaches. It is distinctive in this respect among all the Mahayana sutras, that even a female can become, and become immediately, a Buddha. Whether the chapter is an interpolation or not, it has had a profound effect on Mahayana doctrine and propagation.

XIII

THE King of Healing and another great Bodhisattva named Eloquent, are now introduced. Whether they are creations from the author's own imagination, or of a preceding age is not known. The two seek to allay the Buddha's anxiety in regard to the future of the Lotus Doctrine in this realm of Sakyamuni's Buddhaship.

"Be pleased, World-honoured One, to be without anxiety! After the extinction of the Buddha we will keep, read, recite, and preach this Sutra. In the evil age to come, living beings will decrease in good qualities and increase in utter arrogance, coveting gain and honours, developing their evil qualities and being far removed from deliverance. Though it may be difficult to teach and convert them, we, exerting our utmost patience, will read and recite this Sutra, keep, preach, and copy it, pay every kind of homage to it, and be unsparing of body and life."

Companies of disciples also approach to take the same vow. They are followed by the Buddha's aunt, who was also his foster-mother. Standing before him with her six thousand nuns, she gazes into his face silently. In reply to her appealing look he says:

"Why, with sad countenance, do you gaze at the Tathagata? Are you not thinking that I have not mentioned your name nor predicted you to Perfect

176

Enlightenment? Gautami! I have already inclusively announced that the future of all my disciples is predicted. Now you, who desire to know your future destiny, shall in the worlds to come become a great Teacher in the law of sixty-eight thousand kotis of Buddhas. And these your six thousand bikshunis, still in training and already trained, will become teachers of the Law. Thus you will gradually become perfect in the Bodhisattva-Way, and will become a Buddha entitled 'Loveliness' Tathagata."

To Rahula's mother is promised similarly the title of "The Perfect Myriad-rayed Tathagata". These two and all their followers rejoice with great joy, and take the vow to preach the Lotus Truth.

After these the vast assembly of Great Bodhisattvas, who may be described as the angels and archangels of Buddhism, approach the Buddha and with folded hands, reflect thus:

"If the World-honoured One commands us to keep and expound this Sutra, we will proclaim abroad this Law as the Buddha has taught it." Again they reflect thus: "The Buddha now is silent; we are not commanded. What shall we do?"

"Then these Bodhisattvas, respectfully obeying the Buddha's will and themselves desiring to fulfil their original vow, before the Buddha raise a lion's roar and utter a vow saying: 'World-honoured One! After the extinction of the Tathagata we will compass and travel through the worlds in every direction, in order to lead all the living to copy this Sutra, receive and keep, read and recite it, expound its meaning, practise it as their law, and rightly keep it in mind; entirely by the Buddha's might. Be pleased, World-honoured One, though in another quarter, to behold and guard us from afar!'"

The whole company now chant together a long poem from which the following stanzas are taken. It will be observed that the author shows he has already experienced the rejection of the new doctrine at the hands of the orthodox. He reveals his resentment against the Hinayanists in various ways, and especially against their calumny that his Sutra has been invented for gain or fame and to delude the people.

"Pray be without anxiety!
After the Buddha's extinction,
In the last dread evil age,
We will proclaim this Sutra.
Though many ignorant men
Will with evil mouth abuse us,
And beat us with swords and staves,
We will endure it all.
Monks in that evil age,
Heretical, warped, suspicious,
Crying 'attained' when they have not,
Will have minds full of arrogance.
Others in the Aranya
Will wear the patched robe in seclusion,
Thinking they walk the true path,
And scorning dwellers among men.

178

Others greedy for gain,
Will preach the Law to laymen
And be revered by the world as Arhats
Of the Six Transcendent Powers;
These men cherishing evil minds,
Ever thinking of earthly things,
Assuming the name of Aranyas,
Will love to calumniate us,
Saying such words as these—
'All these bhikshu-fellows,
Because of love of gain,
Preach an heretical doctrine;
Themselves have composed this Sutra
To delude the people of the world;
For the sake of acquiring fame,
They specialize on this Sutra.'
Always in the assemblies,
In order that they may ruin us,
To kings and to their ministers,
To Brahmans and to citizens,
To the other groups of bhikshus,
Of us they will speak slanderously,
Saying: 'These are men of false views,
Who proclaim heretical doctrines.'
    But, from reverence for Buddha,
We will endure those evils.
Though contemptuously addressed as—
'All you Buddhas!'
Even such scorn and arrogance
We will patiently endure.
In the corrupt kalpa's evil age.

Abounding in fear and dread,
Devils will take possession of them
To curse, abuse and insult us.
But we, reverently believing Buddha,
Will wear the armour of long-suffering;
For the sake of preaching this Sutra
Every hard thing we will endure.
We will not love body nor life,
But care only for the Supreme Way."

And again:

"In the presence of the World-honoured One
And the Buddhas from every direction,
Thus we make our vows,
And the Buddha knows our hearts."

XIV

THE great Bodhisattva Manjuśri now addresses the Buddha in praise of this vast concourse, which has pledged itself wholly and solely to The Lotus doctrine. He asks how they are to preach it in the evil age to come. Thereupon the Buddha lays down certain rules, which are styled the Four Methods.

The first is styled the Bodhisattva's Sphere of Action and Intimacy; the second, that of a Serene Mind; the third, that of Thought towards Others; and the fourth, that of Charity and Compassion.

In the Sphere of Action and Intimacy, the bodhisattva "dwells in a state of patience, is gentle and agreeable, is neither hasty nor overbearing, and his mind is unperturbed; he has no active interest in affairs, but sees all things in their reality, and neither takes part in nor discusses them". As to his intimates, he has no intimacy with kings, princes, ministers, and rulers; nor with heretics and naked fakirs; nor with authors of worldly books of prose or poetry; nor with pugilists, sportsmen and jugglers; nor with hunters, fishermen and butchers; nor with keepers of domestic animals for food. He may preach the Law to them when they seek him, expecting nothing in return. His objection to Hinayana is so strong that he will not consort with its disciples, nor speak to them, neither within nor without. If they should come to him, he preaches the Sutra to them.

He is strict in conduct towards women and girls. He should not "preach the Law to women, displaying an appearance capable of arousing passionate thoughts, nor have pleasure in seeing them; if he enters the homes of others, he does not converse with any girl, virgin, widow, and so forth, nor again does he become on friendly terms with any hermaphrodite; he does not enter the homes of others alone; if for some reason he must enter there alone, then with single mind he thinks on the Buddha; if he preaches the Law to women, he does not show his teeth in smiles, nor let his breast be seen; not even for the sake of the Law does he ever become intimate with them, how much less for other reasons. He takes no pleasure in keeping young pupils, sramaneras, and children; nor has he pleasure in being with them as teachers; but ever preferring meditation and seclusion, he cultivates and controls his mind. Manjuśri! This is termed the first Intimate Sphere of a Bodhisattva".

His proper sphere of Intimacy is with things in their reality. He looks upon them as empty, void, unreal and thus sees them as they really are, "just like space, of the nature of nothingness, cut off from the course of all words and expressions, unborn, not coming forth, not arising, nameless, formless, really without existence, infinite, boundless, unimpeded, unrestrained, only existing in causation and brought into being through perceptive perversion."

"If any Bodhisattva
In the future evil age
With fearlessness of mind
Desires to preach this Sutra,
Let him occupy his Sphere of Action
And his proper Sphere of Intimacy;
Ever avoiding kings,
And the sons of kings,
Ministers and rulers,
Brutal and dangerous performers.

. . . . . .

Let him also not consort
With men of arrogance
Devoted to the study of the
Tripitaka of Hinayana.

. . . . . .

Nor with female disciples
Fond of banter and laughter.

. . . . . .

But if such people as these,
In goodness of their mind,
Come to the Bodhisattva
To hear the Buddha-Way
Then the Bodhisattva,
With fearless of mind,
Cherishing no expectation,
Should preach to them the Law.

. . . . . .

If there should be any monk
Who, after my extinction,

183

Enters this Sphere of Action
And this Sphere of Intimacy,
When he preaches this Sutra,
He will be freed from timid weakness.
When this Bodhisattva
Enters his quiet room,
And, in perfect meditation,
Sees things in their true meaning,
And, rising from his meditation,
Whether to kings or nations,
Or princes, ministers and people,
To Brahmans or to others,
Opens up, expounds,
And preaches to them this Sutra,
His mind shall be at ease
And free from timid weakness.
Manjuśri!
This is the Bodhisattva's
First Law of Steadfastness,
By which he is able, in future ages,
To preach the Law-Flower Sutra."

The second Sphere is that of Serenity. In preaching he has no pleasure in exposing the errors of
others, or of the Sutras; he despises not other
preachers, nor speaks of their good or evil, their
merits or demerits; nor does he single out disciples
by name and expose their sins, nor by name praise
their virtues; nor does he cherish dislike. By keeping well such a serene heart, those who hear will
not oppose him. "To those who ask difficult questions, he does not give answer after the manner of

the Hinayanists, but in Mahayana fashion, explaining in such manner that they may obtain Perfect Knowledge."

> "The wise man in ways such as these,
>   Rightly cultivates his mind,
>   And is able to abide serene.
>   The merit of such a man,
>   Thousands, myriads, kotis of kalpas
>   Spent in reckoning and comparison
>   Would not suffice for the telling."

The Third Sphere is that of his attitude of mind towards others; but it is not easy to distinguish this Sphere from the last. He "does not cherish an envious, suspicious and deceitful mind; nor does he slight and abase the learners of the Buddha-Way and seek out their excesses and shortcomings". He does not distress any seekers, causing them doubts and regrets. He does not indulge in disputations. He is reverent to the Buddhas and Bodhisattvas and preaches the Law, neither more nor less. Nothing can perturb such a monk and multitudes will flock to hear him.

> "Let him who would preach the Sutra
>   Renounce an envious, angry, proud,
>   Deceitful or false mind,
>   And ever do upright deeds;
>   He should disparage none,
>   Never argue over the Law,
>   Nor cause others doubts or regret,

. . . . . .

But ever be gentle, patient,
And compassionate to all."

The Fourth Sphere of Action is that of Charity towards laymen and friars, and Compassion for those not yet bodhisattvas. He should remember that these people are great losers, for they have never learnt the true Way. "Though they have not sought, nor believed, nor understood this Sutra", yet, says the Buddha, "when I have attained to my Perfect Enlightenment, wherever I am, by my transcendent powers and powers of wisdom, I will lead them to take up their abode in this Law."

The disciple who reaches and accomplishes the Fourth Sphere, when he preaches will be free from error, and will ever be revered by all disciples, kings and princes, ministers and people, brahmans and citizens. The gods will protect him and will reveal to him the answer to those who confront him with hard questions; because this Sutra is that which all Buddhas, past, present, and to come, watch over by their divine powers.

Then follows a parable to show that it is the very jewel of jewels, the crown-jewel of the Buddhas.

"It is like a powerful sacred Wheel-rolling King who desires by force to conquer other domains. When minor kings do not obey his command, the Wheel-rolling King calls up his various armies and goes to punish them. The King, seeing his soldiers distinguish themselves in the war, is greatly pleased and,

according to their merit, bestows rewards, either
giving fields, houses, villages or cities, or giving
garments or personal ornaments, or giving all kinds
of treasures, gold, silver, lapis lazuli, moon-stones,
agates, coral, amber, elephants, horses, carriages,
litters, male and female slaves, and people; only the
crown-jewel on his head he gives to none. Wherefore? Because only on the head of a king may this
sole jewel be worn, and, if he were to give it, his
retinue would be amazed. Manjuśri! The Tathagata
is also like this. By his powers of meditation and
wisdom, he has taken possession of the domain of the
Law and rules as King over the triple world. But
the Mara-kings are unwilling to submit. The Tathagata's wise and holy generals fight against them. With
those who distinguish themselves he, too, is pleased,
and in the midst of his four hosts preaches the Sutras
to them, causing them to rejoice, bestowing on them
the meditations, the emancipations, the faultless roots
and powers, and all the wealth of the Law. In addition, he gives them the city of Nirvana, saying that
they have attained to extinction, and attracts their
minds so that they all rejoice; yet he does not yet
preach to them this Law-Flower Sutra. Manjuśri!
Just as the Wheel-rolling King, seeing his soldiers
distinguish themselves, is so extremely pleased that
now at last he gives them the incredible jewel so long
worn on his head, which may not wantonly be given
to any one, so also is it with the Tathagata.

"As the Great Law-King of the triple world,
teaching and converting the living by his Law,

when he sees his wise and holy army fighting with
the Mara of the five mental processes, the Mara of
earthly ills, and the Mara of death, and doing so with
great exploits and merits, exterminating the three
poisons, escaping from the triple world, and breaking
through the nets of the Maras, then the Tathagata
also is greatly pleased. Now at last he preaches this
Law-Flower Sutra which has never before been
preached, and which is able to cause all the living to
reach perfect knowledge, though the world greatly
resents and has difficulty in believing it. Manjuśri!
This Law-Flower Sutra is the supreme teaching of
the Tathagatas and the most profound of all discourses. I give it to you last, just as that powerful
king at last gives the brilliant jewel he has guarded
for long. Manjuśri! This Law-Flower Sutra is the
mysterious treasury of the Buddha-Tathagatas, which
is supreme above all Sutras. For long has it been
guarded and not prematurely declared; to-day for
the first time I proclaim it to you."

"It is like to a powerful
 Wheel-rolling King
 Who, to his war-distinguished soldiers,
 Makes presents of many rewards,
 Elephants, horses, carriages,
 Litters, personal ornaments,
 As well as fields and houses,
 Villages and cities;
 Or bestows garments,
 Various kinds of jewels,
 Slaves and other wealth,

Bestowing all with joy;
But only for one, heroic
And of rare exploits,
Does the king take from his head
The crown-jewel to give him.
   Thus also is it with the Tathagata;
He is the king of the laws,
Possessing great powers of endurance
And the treasury of wisdom;
With great benevolence,
He transforms the world with his Law
Seeing every human being
Suffering from pains and distresses,
Seeking for deliverance,
Fighting against the Maras,
To these living beings,
He has preached various laws
And, in great tactfulness,
Has preached these numerous Sutras;
Finally knowing the living
Have attained developed powers,
At the very last he to them
Preaches this Law-Flower,
As the king takes from his head
The jewel and bestows it.
So this Sutra is pre-eminent
Among all the Sutras.
   I have always carefully guarded
And not prematurely revealed it.
Now, indeed, is the time
To preach it to you all.

After my extinction,
Whoever seeks Buddhahood
And desires in serenity
To proclaim this Sutra,
Should associate himself with
Such four rules as these.
   He who reads this Sutra
Will ever be free from worry
And free from pain and disease;
His face will be fresh and white;
He will not be born poor,
In low estate, or ugly.
All creatures will delight to see him
As of a longed-for saint;
Heavenly cherubim
Will be his servitors.
Nor sword, nor staff, will be làid on him;
Poison cannot harm him;
If any one would curse him,
That man's mouth will be closed.
Fearlessly he will roam
Like to a Lion-king.
The radiance of his wisdom
Will shine forth like the sun.
If he should be in dreams,
He will only behold the wonderful,
Seeing the Tathagatas
Seated on Lion-Thrones,
Preaching the Law to hosts
Of surrounding bhikshus.

.   .   .   .   .

He will also see the Buddhas,
With the sign of the golden body,
Emitting boundless light,
Illuminating all beings,
And with their Brahma-voices,
Discoursing on the laws.
While Buddha to the four groups
Is preaching the Supreme Law,
He will find himself in the midst
Praising Buddha with folded hands;
Hearing the Law with joy."

XV

THE Great Bodhisattvas, numerous as the sands of Ganges, who had come from other Buddha-realms, now offer their services to Śakyamuni Buddha in his realm. But to them he replies that he already has vast numbers of Great Bodhisattvas of his own.

"Enough! My good sons! There is no need for you to protect and keep this Sutra. Wherefore? Because in my Saha-world there are in fact Bodhisattva-Mahasattvas as the sands of sixty thousand Ganges; each one of these Bodhisattvas has a retinue as the sands of sixty thousand Ganges; these persons are able, after my extinction, to protect and keep, read and recite, and preach abroad this Sutra."

"When the Buddha has thus spoken, the earth of the Three-Thousand-Great-Thousandfold Land of the Saha-world trembles and quakes and from its midst there issue together innumerable thousands, myriads, kotis of Bodhisattva-Mahasattvas. All these Bodhisattvas with their golden-hued bodies, thirty-two Signs, and boundless radiance, have before been dwelling below this Saha-world, in the space supporting this world. These Bodhisattvas, hearing the voice of Śakyamuni Buddha preaching, spring forth from below. Each one of them is the commander of a great host, each leading a retinue as the sands of the sixty thousand Ganges; moreover, others lead their retinues as the sands of fifty thousand, forty thousand, thirty thousand, twenty thousand, ten thousand Ganges, down to the sands of one Ganges, the sands of half a Ganges, a quarter of it, down to a fraction of it, the decimal point of thousands, myriads, kotis of nayutas; moreover, a thousand myriad kotis of nayutas of followers, a myriad kotis of followers, a thousand myriad, a hundred, or even ten; moreover, those who lead five, four, three, two disciples, or even one disciple; moreover, one who is alone, happy in the practice of isolation. Such Bodhisattvas as these are immeasurable, illimitable, beyond the powers of comprehension by calculation or comparison.

"When these Bodhisattvas have emerged from the earth, each goes up to the wonderful Stupa of the Precious Seven in the sky, where are the Tathagata Abundant-Treasures and Śakyamuni Buddha. On their arrival they make obeisance with faces to the ground towards both the World-honoured Ones and, going to the Buddhas seated on the lion-thrones under the jewel-trees, they also salute them, three times making procession round them on their right, with folded hands revering them, and extolling them with all kinds of Bodhisattva hymns. Then they stand on one side, with delight gazing upon both the World-honoured Ones.

"From the time that these Bodhisattva-Mahasattvas first issue from the earth and extol the Buddhas with all kinds of Bodhisattva hymns, in the interval there pass fifty minor kalpas. During this time Śakyamuni Buddha sits in silence; silent also are the four groups; but the fifty kalpas, through the divine power of the Buddha, seem to the great multitude as but half a day."

The four leaders of this vast host then ask the Buddha:

"Is the World-honoured One at ease,
With few ailments and troubles?
In instructing the living beings,
Is he free from weariness?
And are all the living
Readily accepting his teaching?
Do they not cause the World-honoured
To become weary and tired?"

"Yes! Yes! My good sons!" replies the Buddha, "The Tathagata is at ease, with few ailments and few troubles. These beings are easy to convert and transform and I am free from weariness. . . . All these beings from first seeing me and hearing my preaching, have received it in faith, and entered the Tathagata-wisdom, save those who had practised and learnt the Hinayana; but even such as these I have now caused to hear this Sutra and enter the Buddha-Wisdom."

The Bodhisattvas reply:

"Good! Good!
Great Hero, World-honoured One!
All these living creatures
Are easily transformed by thee,
Are able to inquire into
The profound wisdom of Buddhas
And, hearing, to believe and discern.
We therefore felicitate thee."

Maitreya and the disciples are amazed at this vast concourse, and at Śakyamuni claiming them as his Bodhisattvas.

> "These countless thousands, myriads,
> This great host of Bodhisattvas,
> We have never seen their like.
> Be pleased to tell, honoured of men,
> Whence came they and why
> They are thus assembled
> Mighty of frame, transcendent in power,
> Of wisdom inscrutable,
> Strong of will and memory,
> Firm in endurance,
> Whom all rejoice to see—
> Whence came they?"

A long account follows descriptive of their countless numbers:

> "If any one tried to keep tally
> Through kalpas as Ganges' sands
> He still could not tell their number.
> All these great, majestic,
> Zealous Bodhisattva hosts—
> Who has preached the Law to them,
> Instructed and perfected them?
>
> . . . . . .
>
> From every quarter of the riven earth
> They all spring forth from its midst.
> World-honoured One! From of old
> We have never witnessed such beings.
>
> . . . . . .

We know not a single one
Among this countless host,
Who suddenly spring from the earth.
Be pleased to tell us the cause!

.   .   .   .   .

What is the course of their history?
World-honoured One of measureless Virtue
Wilt thou resolve our doubts?"

In like manner the disciples of the concourse of
other Buddhas present, each asks his own Buddha
the same question: This vast concourse of the
glorified—whence came they?

"Good, good! Ajita!" replies Śakyamuni to Maitreya,
"Well have you asked the Buddha concerning so
great a matter. Do you all, with one mind, don the
armour of zeal and exhibit a firm will, for the Tathagata now intends to reveal and proclaim the wisdom
of Buddhas, the sovereign and supernatural power of
Buddhas, the lion-eagerness of Buddhas, and the awe-
inspiring forceful power of Buddhas."

Then first in prose, afterwards in verse Maitreya
is told:

"Ajita! Know thou!
These Great Bodhisattvas,
Who, from past numberless kalpas,
Have observed the Buddha wisdom,
All of these are my converts,
Whose minds I have set on the Great Way.
These Bodhisattvas are my sons
Who dwell in this Buddha-world.

9. Kuan-yin, the Regarder of the Cries of the world, saves the
storm-tossed mariners who call for aid

From an A. D. 1681 facsimile of an A. D. 1331 edition of the illustrated
Kuan-yin chapter of this Sutra

Ever practising the Dhuta deeds,
Joyfully devoted to quiet places,
Shunning the clamour of crowds,
With no pleasure in many words.
All these sons of mine,
Learning and keeping the Law of my Way,
Are always zealous day and night,
For the sake of seeking Buddhahood;
They dwell below the Saha-world,
In the region of space beneath it.
Firm in their powers of will and memory,
Ever diligent in seeking wisdom,
They preach every kind of mystic law,
Their minds devoid of any fear.
I, near the city of Gaya,
Sitting beneath the Bodhi-tree,
Accomplished Perfect Enlightenment;
And rolling the supreme Law-wheel,
I then taught and converted them
And caused them to seek the One Way.
Now they all abide in the never-relapsing state,
And every one will become a Buddha.
What I now speak is the truth;
Believe it with single mind!
I from a long distant past
Have taught and trained all this host."

Maitreya and the disciples again express their perplexity, wondering how the Master can have instructed such a countless host in so short a time.
They remind him that but forty years have passed
since his own enlightenment under the bodhi-tree.

How can he have accomplished such mighty Buddha-deeds in so brief a period? If the host were counted through all time, their numbers could not be told. These Bodhisattvas are not beings of earth, but have lived through the far past under countless numbers of Buddhas.

"World-honoured One! Such a claim the world will find it hard to credit.

"It is much as if there were a man, of fine complexion and black hair, twenty-five years old, who pointed to centenarians and said: 'These are my sons'; and as if these centenarians also pointed to the youth and said: 'This is our father who begot and reared us'. This matter is hard of belief. So also is it with the Buddha, whose attainment of the Way is truly not long since. Yet this great host of Bodhisattvas, for numberless, thousands, myriads, kotis of kalpas, for the sake of Buddahood, have devoted themselves with zeal; they have entered deep into, come out of and dwelt in infinite hundreds, thousands, myriads, kotis of samadhis; have attained the great transcendent faculties and for long lived noble lives; have been well able, step by step, to learn all kinds of good laws; they are skilful in question and answer, are treasures amongst men and of extreme rareness in all the world. Yet to-day the World-honoured One has just said that, when he attained to Buddhahood, he then caused them to set their minds on enlightenment, instructed and led, and caused them to proceed toward Perfect Enlightenment. It is not long since the World-honoured One became a Buddha, yet he has been able to do this great meritorious deed! Though we ourselves still believe that what the Buddha has opportunely preached, and the words the Buddha has uttered, have never been false, and also the Buddha's knowledge is all perceived by us, yet if newly-converted bodhisattvas hear this statement after the Buddha's extinction, they may not believe it, with resultant misdeeds, to the destruction of the Law. So, World-honoured One, be pleased to explain it, removing our doubts so that thy good sons in future generations, on hearing this matter, shall also not beget doubt."

> "We ourselves believe the Buddha
> And have no doubts upon this matter;
> But beg the Buddha, for future hearers,
> To explain, that they may understand.
> For if any in regard to this Sutra
> Should beget unbelief and doubt,
> He would fall into evil karma.
> Be pleased to make explanation
> How these numberless Bodhisattvas
> In so short a space of time,
> Have been instructed and developed,
> And abide in this ever-advancing stage."

XVI

In reply to these questions Śakyamuni now makes his great revelation. This chapter is the climax. It contains the author's declaration that the Buddha is Eternal, beyond all limits of time and space. It is the Eternal Buddha who is in Sakyamuni. His is the voice that speaks, His the vast host, His the Eternal Life which gives its name to this chapter.

Then says the Buddha to the Bodhisattvas and the vast assembly:

"Believe and discern, all you good sons, the Tathagata's word of Truth."

Thrice he repeats it.

Maitreya, with folded hands, implores the Buddha, and all the disciples cry with him three times,

"We beseech thee explain; we will believe the Buddha's word."

"Then the World-honoured, perceiving that the bodhisattvas thrice without ceasing repeated their request, addressed them saying:

" 'Listen then each of you attentively to the secret, mysterious and supernatural power of Tathagata. All the worlds of gods, men and asuras declare: "Now has Śakyamuni-Buddha, coming forth from the palace of the Sakya-clan, and seated at the place of enlightenment, not far from the city of Gaya, attained to Perfect Enlightenment." But, good sons, since

I veritably became Buddha, there have passed infinite, boundless, hundreds, thousands, myriads, kotis, nayutas of kalpas. For instance, suppose there were five hundred thousand myriad kotis, nayutas of numberless Three-Thousand-Great-Thousandfold-Worlds; let some one grind them to atoms, pass eastward through five hundred thousands, myriads, kotis, nayutas of numberless countries, and then drop one of those atoms; suppose he thus proceeded eastward till he had finished those atoms,—what do you think, good sons, is it possible to imagine and calculate all those worlds so as to know their number?'

. . . . . .

"'Good sons! Now I must clearly announce and declare to you. Suppose you take as atomized all those worlds, everywhere that an atom has been deposited, and everywhere that it has not been deposited, and count an atom as a kalpa, the time since I became the Buddha still surpasses these by hundreds, thousands, myriads, kotis, nayutas of numberless kalpas. From that time forward I have constantly been preaching and teaching in this Saha-world, and also leading and benefitting the living in other places in hundreds, thousands, myriads, kotis, nayutas of numberless domains. Good sons! During this time, I have spoken of the Buddha "Burning Light" and other Buddhas, and also have told of their entering Nirvana. Thus have I tactfully described them all. Good sons! Whenever living beings came to me, I beheld with a Buddha's eyes all the faculties, keen or dull, of their faith, and so forth;

and I explained to them, in stage after stage, according to their capacity and degree of salvation, my different names and the length of my lives, and moreover plainly stated that I must enter Nirvana. I also, with various expedients, preached the Wonderful Law which is able to cause the living to beget a joyful heart. Good sons! Beholding the propensities of all the living towards lower things, so that they have little virtue and much vileness, to these the Tathagata declares: 'I, in my youth, left home and attained to Perfect Enlightenment.' But since I veritably became Buddha, thus have I ever been, only by my expedient methods teaching and transforming all the living, so that they may enter into Buddhahood, and thus have I made declaration.

"Good sons! All the sutras which the Tathagata preaches are for the deliverance of the living—whether they speak of himself or speak of others, whether they indicate himself or others, and whether they indicate his own affairs or those of others; whatever they say is all real, and not empty air. Wherefore? Because the Tathagata knows and sees the character of the triple world as it really is; to him there is neither birth nor death, neither going away nor coming forth; neither existence in the world nor cessation of existence; neither reality nor unreality; neither thus nor otherwise. Unlike the way the triple world beholds the triple world, the Tathagata sees clearly such things as these without mistake. Because all the living have various natures, various desires, various activities, various ideas and reasonings, so, desiring to cause them to produce the roots of goodness, the Tathagata by so many reasonings, parables, and discourses has preached his various Truths. The Buddha-deeds which he performs never fail for a moment. Thus it is, since I became Buddha in the far distant past, that my lifetime is of numberless kalpas, forever existing and immortal.

"Good sons! The lifetime which I fulfil in following the Bodhisattva-Way is not even yet completed, but will be again twice the previous number of kalpas. But now in this unreal Nirvana, I announce that I must enter the real Nirvana. In this expedient way the Tathagata teaches all living. Wherefore? If the Buddha abides long in the world, men of little virtue—who do not cultivate the roots of goodness and are spiritually poor and mean, greedily attached to the five desires, and caught in the net of wrong reflection and false views—if they see the Tathagata constantly present and not extinct, will become puffed up and lazy, and unable to conceive the idea that it is difficult to meet a Buddha, and be unable to develop a mind of reverence for him. Therefore the Tathagata tactfully says: "Know, Bhikshus! The appearance of a Buddha in the world is a rare occurrence." Wherefore? In the course of countless hundreds, thousands, myriads, kotis of kalpas, some men of little virtue may happen to see a Buddha, or none may see him. For this reason I say: "Bhikshus! A Tathagata may rarely be seen!" All these living beings, hearing such a statement, must indeed realize the thought of the difficulty of meeting a Buddha and cherish a longing and a thirst for him; thus will they cultivate the roots of goodness. Therefore the Tathagata, though he does not in reality become extinct, yet announces his extinction.'"

The Parable of the Physician.

"Suppose, for instance, a good physician, who is wise and perspicacious, conversant with the medical art, and skilful in healing all sorts of diseases. He has many sons, say ten, twenty, even up to a hundred. Because of some matter he goes abroad to a distant country. After his departure his sons drink his poisonous medicines, which send them into a delirium and they lie rolling on the ground. At this moment their father comes back to his home. Of the sons who drank the poison, some have lost their senses, others are still sensible and, on seeing their father approaching in the distance, they are greatly delighted, and kneeling greet him:

"'How good it is that you are returned in safety! We, in our foolishness, have mistakenly dosed ourselves with poison. We beg that you will heal us and give us back our lives.'

"The father, seeing his sons in such distress, in accordance with his prescriptions, seeks for good herbs, perfect in colour, scent and fine flavour, and then pounds, sifts, and mixes them and gives them to his sons to take, saying thus:

"'This excellent medicine with colour, scent and fine flavour all perfect, do you take, and it will at once rid you of your distress so that you will have no more suffering.'

"Those amongst the sons who are sensible, seeing this excellent medicine with colour and scent both good, take it immediately and are wholly delivered from their illness. The others who have lost their senses, seeing their father come, though they are also delighted, salute him and ask him to heal their illness, yet when he offers them the medicine, they are unwilling to take it. Wherefore? Because the poison has entered deeply, they have lost their senses, and even in regard to this medicine of excellent colour and scent they say that it is not good. The father reflects thus:

"'Alas! for these sons, afflicted by this poison, and their minds all unbalanced! Though they are glad to see me and implore for healing, yet they are unwilling to take such excellent medicine as this. Now I must arrange an expedient plan so that they will take this medicine.'

"Then he says to them: 'Know, all of you, that I am now worn out with old age and that the time of my death has arrived. This excellent medicine I now leave here. You may take it and have no fear of not being better.' After thus admonishing them, he departs again for another country and sends a messenger back to inform them: 'Your father is dead.' And now, when these sons hear that their father is dead, their minds are greatly distressed and they thus reflect: 'If our father were alive, he would have pity on us, and we should be saved and preserved. But now he has left us and died in a distant country.'

"Deeming themselves orphans with no one to rely

on, continuous grief brings them to their senses; they recognize the colour, scent and excellent flavour of the medicine, and thereupon take it, when their poisoning is entirely relieved. Their father, hearing that the sons are recovered, seeks an opportunity and returns, showing himself to them all.

" ' Good sons! What is your opinion? Are there any who could say that this good physician has committed the sin of falsehood?' "

The verse portion is much briefer than the prose, and contains only a part of the teaching. The following is a selection from it.

"In order to save all creatures,
  I expediently speak of Nirvana,
  Yet truly I am not extinct,
  But ever here preaching the Law.
  I ever remain in this world,
  In supernatural power,
  So that all perverted creatures
  Fail to see me, though near,
  Looking on me as extinct,
  Everywhere worshipping my relics,
  Cherishing desire for goodness
  And thirsting with aspiration.
  When all creatures have submitted,
  Are upright, and gentle in mind,
  Whole-heartedly looking for Buddha,
  Not caring for their own lives,
  Then I with all the Samgha
  On the Spirit Vulture-Peak appear,

And then I tell all creatures
That I exist here forever undying,
By means of expedients revealing
Myself as dead, yet not dead.
If in other regions there are beings,
Reverent and joying in faith,
Again I am in their midst
To preach the Supreme Law.
You, not hearing of this,
Only say I am extinct.
I, beholding all living creatures
Sunk in the sea of suffering,
At first do not show myself,
But set them expectant and thirsting,
Then, when their hearts are longing,
I appear to preach the Law.
In supernatural power,
Through kalpas numberless
On the Spirit Vulture-Peak am I,
And in other dwelling-places.
While the living see, at the kalpa's end,
The conflagration in its burning,
Tranquil remains this realm of mine,
Ever full of gods and men,
Parks and many palaces
With every sort of gem adorned,
Blooming and fruitful jewel trees,
Where all creatures pleasure take;
The gods strike up their heavenly drums
And music make for evermore,
Showering down celestial flowers

On Buddha and His mighty host.
My Pure Land is not destroyed,
Though all view it as being burnt up,
And grief and horror and distress
Thus fill them to the full.
Those creatures, full of sin
By reason of their evil karma,
Through kalpas numberless hear not
The name of the most Precious Three.
But those who virtuous deeds shall do,
Are gentle and of upright nature,
These will ever me behold
Here expounding to all the Law.
At times unto this eager throng
I preach the Buddha's eternal life."

And, lastly:

"Like the physician who, with clever device
In order to cure his demented sons,
Though indeed alive, announces his death,
Yet none is able to charge him with falsehood.
I, too, being Father of this world,
Who heal all misery and affliction,
For the sake of the perverted people,
Though truly alive, say I am extinct;
Lest, because they always see me,
They should arrogant minds beget,
Be dissolute, set in their five desires,
And fall into karma-paths of ill."

XVII

DURING the length of time that the Buddha tells of the eternity of his life, vast hosts, numerous as sands of Ganges, attain to the assurance of no further re-incarnation; others attain powers of hearing and keeping the Law; others powers of eloquence and argument; others of insight into infinite motion; others of preaching the Law; others, after various stages, of Perfect Enlightenment. The numbers given for each group are as the atoms of various kinds and numbers of worlds.

While the Buddha is telling of the eternity of his life, on the host of Buddhas seated on their lion-thrones beneath the jewel-trees and on their retinues, on the Bodhisattvas and their retinues, and on the assembly, there rain down celestial flowers and fine incense. In the heavens the celestial drums resound with deep reverberation. Celestial robes, jewels, necklaces, censers burning priceless incense, descend upon the congregation. Celestial canopies arise high as the Brahma-heavens; and countless Bodhisattvas sing praises to the Buddhas.

Maitreya then arises from his seat and repeats this, in lengthy verse.

"The Buddha has preached the rare Law
Never heard by us before.
Great is the power of the World-honoured,
And His lifetime beyond estimation.

·   ·   ·   ·   ·

With thousands, myriads of stanzas
The Buddha's praise is sung.

.   .   .   .   .

Learning the Buddha's life is limitless
All creatures are filled with joy,
The Buddha's fame sounds through the Universe,
Enriching all the roots
Of goodness of the living,
To bring them to the Supreme Truth."

The Buddha then proceeds to say that those who have heard and believed, however feebly, his truth of the Eternal Life of the Buddha, have merit surpassing the merit of works.

"Suppose," he says, "there be any good son or daughter who, to obtain Perfect Enlightenment, during eight hundred thousand kotis of nayutas of kalpas, puts in practice the Five Paramitas . . . these merits, compared with the above-mentioned merit, are not equal to even the hundredth part, the thousandth part, or indeed one part of a hundred thousand myriad kotis of it; indeed neither numbers nor comparison can make it known. If any good son or daughter possesses only such merit of faith, there is no such thing as failing to obtain Perfect Enlightenment."

The verse part is still more elaborate in its comparison of the respective values of faith and works. Though a man should live the most devoted life and sacrifice everything—

"Yet, any good son or daughter
Who hears me declare my Eternity,
And believes with a single thought,
This one's reward surpasses his.

        .   .   .   .   .

Just as the present World-honoured One
Who, King of all the Sakyas,
On his Wisdom-Throne raised the Lion's roar,
And fearlessly preached the Law,
So may we, in future ages,
Honoured and revered by all,
Sit on the Wisdom throne
And tell of long life in like manner."

If any have faith in the Eternal Life of the Buddha,
he will see the Buddha always on the Spiritual
Vulture Peak surrounded by the celestial host ever
preaching this Law. He will see, too, the realm in
which he lives resplendent with palaces and jewels.
But he who devotes himself to this Sutra will have
joys even greater. Such a one carries the Tathagata
on his head, or as we may say, is crowned with the
Tathagata.

"Such a good son or daughter need no more erect
stupas, temples or monasteries for me, or make offerings to the monks."

The implication is that such a one, himself or her-
self, is the shrine or temple of the living Buddha.
The narrative shows that faith is works—

"By reason of devotion to the Lotus Sutra, he or she

has in effect already erected stupas, built monasteries, and made offerings to the monks; that is to say, has spiritually erected for the Buddha's relics, stupas of the Precious Seven, high and broad, and tapering up to the Brahma-heaven, with flags and canopies and precious bells, and with flowers, perfumes, garlands, sandal-powder, unguents, incense, drums, instruments, pipes, flutes, harps, all kinds of dances and plays—singing and lauding with wondrous notes —he or she has already made these offerings for innumerable thousands, myriads, kotis of kalpas.

"Ajita! If any one, after my extinction, hears this Sutra, and is able either to receive and keep, or himself copy, or cause others to copy it, he has already erected monasteries and built red sandal-wood temples of thirty-two shrines, tall as eight Tala-trees, lofty, spacious, splendid, in which abide hundreds, thousands of bhikshus; adorned also with gardens, groves, and bathing-pools, promenades and meditation-cells; with clothing, victuals, bedding, medicaments, and all aids to pleasure provided to the full therein. Such monasteries and such numbers of temples, hundreds, thousands, myriads, kotis, countless in their number, he has here in my presence, offered to me and to my bhikshu-monks. Therefore I say, if any one after the extinction of the Tathagata, receives and keeps, reads and recites it, preaches it to others, either himself copies it, or causes others to copy it, and pays homage to the Sutra, he need no longer erect stupas and temples, or build monasteries, and make offerings to the monks. How much less he who is able to keep this Sutra and thereto add alms-giving, morality, forbearance, zeal, concentration, and wisdom. His merit will be most excellent, infinite and boundless; even as the sky which east, west, south, and north, the four intermediate directions, the zenith and nadir, is infinite and boundless, so also the merit of this man will be infinite and boundless, and he will speedily reach Perfect Knowledge. If any one reads and recites, receives and keeps this Sutra, preaches it to other people, or himself copies it, or causes others to copy it; moreover, is able to erect stupas and build monasteries, and to serve and extol the Sravaka-monks, and also with hundreds, thou-sands, myriads, kotis of ways of extolling, extols the merits of the Bodhisattvas; also if he to other people, with various reasonings, according to its meaning, expounds this Law-Flower Sutra; again, if he is able to keep the commandments in purity, amicably to dwell with the gentle, to endure insult without anger, to be firm in will and thought, ever to value medita-tion, to attain to profound concentration, zealously and boldly to support the good, to be clever and wise in ably answering difficult questionings; Ajita! again, if after my extinction, there be good sons and daugh-ters who receive and keep, read and recite this Sutra, and who possess such excellent merits as these, you may know that those people have proceeded towards the Wisdom-terrace, and are near to Perfect En-lightenment, sitting under the tree of enlightenment. Ajita! Wherever those good sons or good daughters either sit or stand or walk, in that place you should

erect a stupa; all gods and men should pay homage
to it as a stupa of Buddha."

"If any one, after my extinction,
Is able to honour and keep this Sutra,
His happiness will be infinite.

.   .   .   .   .

By this act he has made
Every kind of offering
And erected relic-stupas
Adorned with the precious seven,

.   .   .   .   .

With thousands, myriads of gem-bells
Stirred by the wind to mystic music,
As if for numberless kalpas
He had paid homage to stupas
With flowers, incense, garlands.

.   .   .   .   .

He who is able to keep this Sutra
Will be as if Buddha were present,
And he, with finest sandal-wood,
Built Him monasteries in service,
Built them of thirty-two halls
Eight Tala-trees in height,
With the best of food and garments,
Complete with beds for sleeping,
With rooms for hundreds and thousands,
With gardens, groves and bathing-pools,
With walks and meditation-cells,
All beautifully adorned.

.   .   .   .   .

Whoever does homage to it
Will obtain infinite merit
Boundless as the realms of Space
Such will be his merit.
How much more he who humbly keeps it."

The indwelling Buddha is especially emphasized in
the closing stanzas:

"If one meets with such a teacher,
Strew him with celestial flowers,
Clothe him in divine clothing,
Salute him at his feet
With a mind as if thinking of Buddha.

.   .   .   .   .

Wherever he dwells or stays,
Where he walks, or sits, or lies,
Or speaks but a phrase of the Sutra,
In that place erect a stupa,
Adorn it and make it beautiful,
And in every way pay it homage.
Where'er dwells a Buddha-son,
That place the Buddha uses
And constant within it abides,
And walks and sits and reclines."

XVIII

Maitreya then asks the Buddha what will be the happiness of one who receives with joy the Law-Flower message. The Buddha's reply is that the reward of him who hears, not direct, nor second-hand, but even at fiftieth-hand will be incalculable.

"It is like the number of all the living creatures in the six states of existence in four hundred myriad kotis of numberless worlds, born in the four ways, egg-born, womb-born, humidity-born, or born by metamorphosis, whether they are formed or formless, whether conscious or unconscious, or neither conscious nor unconscious; footless, two-footed, four-footed, or many-footed, it is as the sum of all these living creatures. Suppose some one, seeking their happiness, provides them with every article of pleasure they may desire, giving each creature the whole of a world with its gold, silver, lapis-lazuli, moon-stone, agate, coral, amber, and every sort of wonderful jewel, with elephants, horses, carriages, and palaces, towers built of the Precious Seven—and so forth. This great master of gifts thus bestows gifts for full eighty years and then reflects thus:

"'I have bestowed on all these beings articles of pleasure according to their desires, but now they have grown old and worn, and over eighty years of age, with hair grey and faces wrinkled, and death is not

10. Sudatta spreads the ground of Jeta's garden with bricks of gold, to form the Jetavanavihara as a retreat for the Buddha and his disciples

far off—I ought to instruct and guide them in the Buddha-Law.'

"Thereupon, gathering together those beings, he proclaims to them the Law's instruction; and by his revealing, teaching, benefiting and rejoicing, they all in a moment become disciples . . . free from imperfections, having acquired mastery of profound meditation, and completed the Eight Emancipations. What is your opinion? May the merits obtained by this great master of gifts be considered many or not?"

"World-honoured One!" said Maitreya to the Buddha, "The merits of this man are very many, infinite and boundless. Even though this master of giving had only made gifts of all those articles of pleasure to those creatures, his merits would be infinite; how much more when he causes them to attain to sainthood?'

"Then said the Buddha to Maitreya: 'I will now speak clearly to you. The merits attained by such a man, if he bestowed those means of happiness on all beings in the Six States of existence of four hundred myriad kotis of numberless worlds, and caused them to attain to sainthood, would not compare with the merits of that fiftieth person who, hearing a single verse óf the Law-Flower Sutra, receives it with joy; they are not equal to one hundredth, or one thousandth, or one fraction of a hundred thousand myriad kotis; the power of figures or comparisons cannot express it. Ajita! If the merits of such a fiftieth person who in turn hears the Law-Flower Sutra and accepts it with joy, are indeed so infinite, so boundless and numberless; how much more surpassingly infinite, boundless and beyond number or compare is the happiness of him who is amongst the first hearers in the assembly and receives it joyfully."

If any one hears this preaching even momentarily, his merit is so great that in his next reincarnation "he will acquire the most excellent kind of elephants, horses and carriages, jewelled palanquins and litters, and ride in celestial cars". It is reasonable to accept these as celestial or spiritual ideas, conceived of through the medium of material forms.

Again, if any one invites another to sit down, or share his seat, in order to hear this good news, or persuades another to go and hear it; he will be reborn where wise Bodhisattvas dwell, and himself have all his faculties glorified. His lips will be pure and beautiful, only fragrance will come from them, and his presence will be a joy.

"Age after age his mouth will not suffer,
His teeth not be gaping, yellow or black;
His lips not thick, awry or cracked,
With no disgusting appearance;
His tongue neither dried, black nor shrunk;
His nose high, long and straight;
His forehead broad and smooth;
His face refined and dignified,
A joy for men to behold;
No fetid breath from his mouth,
The scent of the Utpala-flower
Ever exhaling from his lips."

XIX

IF the merits of a hearer are so vast, how much greater those of a preacher of this Sutra! We are told that such a one—and it is interesting to note, whether male or female—will obtain great increase of natural powers, both now and hereafter.

The Buddha is shown as addressing the great Bodhisattva, Ever Zealous. To him he says:

"If any good son or good daughter receives and keeps this Law-Flower Sutra, or reads, or recites, or expounds, or copies it, that person will obtain eight hundred merits of the eye, twelve hundred merits of the ear, eight hundred merits of the nose, twelve hundred merits of the tongue, eight hundred merits of the body, and twelve hundred merits of the mind; with these merits he will dignify his six organs, making them all serene. That good son or good daughter, with serene eyes of flesh, begotten by his parents, will see whatever exists within and without the Three-Thousand-Great-Thousandfold World, mountains, forests, rivers, and seas, down to the Avici hell and up to the summit of existence, and also see the living beings in it, as well as see and know in detail all their karma-causes and re-birth states of retribution."

The twelve hundred merits of the ear are thus described in verse:

"His ears, those begotten by his parents,
Are serene, unsullied, untainted.
By these ordinary ears he hears

The sounds in the Three-Thousand World,
The sounds of elephants, horses, carts, and oxen,
The sounds of gongs, bells, conches, drums,
The sounds of lutes and harps,
The sounds of pipes and flutes,
The sounds of pure lovely song;
Listening without undue attachment,
He hears countless human sounds,
And can understand all he hears;
He hears also the sounds of gods,
And mystic voices of singing;
Hears sounds of men and women,
And sounds of youths and maidens.
In mountains, streams and gorges,
The sounds of Kalavinkas,
Ming-ming and other birds,
All these sounds he hears.
The pangs of the hosts in hell
And all the sounds of their tortures;
Hungry ghosts driven by hunger and thirst
And the sounds of their importunity;
The voices of asuras,
Inhabiting the ocean shores,
When they converse together,
And bellow forth their cries.
Such a preacher as this,
Calmly dwelling here
From afar hears these sounds
Without harm to his organ of hearing.
In the worlds in every direction,
Birds and beasts cry to each other,

And the Preacher here abiding
Hears them in every detail.
All the Brahma heavens above,
From Light-Sound and Universal-Purity
To the Heaven of the Summit of Existence,—
The sounds of their conversation,
The Preacher here abiding,
Hears them in every detail.
All the hosts of bhikshus
And of bhikshunis
Reading or reciting the Sutra,
Or preaching it to others,
The Preacher here abiding
Hears them in every detail.
Also the Bodhisattvas
Who intone this Sutra-Law,
Or preach it unto others,
Collating and expounding its meaning,—
All such sounds as these,
He hears in every detail."

The eight hundred powers of his organ of smell are
so enhanced that, by means of his serene organ, the
fragrance of the world is his. He can also discern
everything by their odour—elephants, cattle, men,
grasses, the gods in their heavens, even Brahma;
"from afar he will smell all these and know where
they abide." Nevertheless, "though he smell these
odours, yet his organ of smell will not be injured, nor
will he make any error; and if he wishes to define
and tell them to others, his meaning will not err."

. . . . .

"The gods, whether walking or seated,
Their rambles and magic powers,
He who keeps this Law-Flower
By smell can know them all.

.   .   .   .   .

Lions, tigers, wolves, elephants,
Bisons, buffaloes and their kind,
He by smell knows their place.
If there be a woman with child,
Who discerns not yet its sex,
Male, female, organless, or inhuman,
He by smell can discern it.
By his power of smell
He knows if the newly pregnant
Will succeed or not in being
Joyfully delivered of happy children.
By his perceptive power of smell
He knows the thoughts of men and women,
Their lusts, foolishness or anger,
And also the maintainers of goodness.
All the hidden treasures,
Gold, silver, and jewels,
Stored in copper vessels,
By smell he can clearly distinguish,
Every kind of jewelled necklace,
Of price beyond all knowledge,
By smell he knows its value,
Its source and its location."

The twelve hundred merits of his tongue are the merits of taste and speech. "Whatever pleasant or unpleasant, sweet or not sweet, bitter or astringent thing meets his tongue will become of the finest flavour, like heavenly nectar; nothing will be unpleasant. If, in the assembly, he uses his organ of the tongue to preach, sonorous and beautiful sounds will enter the hearts of all, giving them pleasure and enjoy." Celestial beings, dragons, demons, monks and nuns, disciples, kings, princes, and ministers, will flock to hear him preach the Law. The Buddhas will delight to hear him and will also preach toward him.

> "If this Preacher desires
> To make his lovely voice
> Fill the whole universe,
> He is able at will to achieve it."

The eight hundred merits of the body not only give him a body clear as crystal which all admire, but to him all other bodies are displayed, for everything of every kind is reflected to him in the crystal mirror of his own body.

"Downward to the Avici-Hell, upward to the Summit of all Existence, all things and all living beings are displayed in his body."

> "As on a pure bright mirror
> Every image is seen,
> So, in his own pure body,
> The Bodhisattva sees the whole world.

. . . . .

'Though not yet possessed of the flawless,
Mystic, spiritual body,
Yet in his pure ordinary body
Everything is revealed."

The twelve hundred merits of thought enable him, "on hearing a single verse or sentence, to penetrate its infinite and boundless meanings. Having discerned those meanings, he will be able to discourse on that single sentence or verse for a month, four months, even a year"—for one verse of this Sutra like "the flower in the crannied wall" opens up vast questions.

"Whatever he ponders, estimates, and speaks, will be the Buddha-Law, nothing but truth, and that which former Buddhas have taught."

"Every living creature
Of this world, within and without,
Gods, dragons, humans,
Yakshas, demons, spirits, others,
These in the six destinations,
Whatever they may be thinking—
In reward for keeping the Law-Flower,
Instant he knows them all.
The countless Buddhas of the universe,
With their hundreds of felicitous signs,
Who preach to all the living,
He hears and retains it all.
He ponders on the infinite,
And preaches the Law without stint,
Never forgets or makes a mistake,

Because he keeps the Law-Flower.
Knowing the form of all laws,
Perceiving their ordered meaning,
Comprehending the terms and words,
He explains them according to knowledge.
Whatever this man preaches
Is the Law of former Buddhas;
And because he proclaims this Law,
He is fearless of the throng.
A keeper of the Law-Flower Sutra
Has an organ of thought such as this.
Though not yet possessed of faultlessness,
Such is the foretoken he possesses."

XX

WE are now introduced to a further interlude, in which the Buddha addresses the great Bodhisattva, Might-Endowed. He tells him of a former Buddha-realm, over which was a Buddha known as King of Majestic Voice. On his entering into Nirvana, his successors followed each other to the number of twenty thousand kotis, each being of the same title. After the Nirvana of the first "Buddha of the Majestic Voice", and after the first period of the pure doctrine had passed, monks of the utmost arrogance obtained the chief power, who cruelly persecuted the hero of the parable that follows. It will be observed that by these the Hinayana School is meant.

That hero is a monk called Never Despise, so styled because he refused to contemn any one, being assured that every one was a prospective buddha. It is a parable of the Mahayanist persecuted by his fellow monks, the Hinayanists, because he preaches universal buddhahood for all the living.

"Might-endowed! For what reason was he named Never Despise? Because he paid respect to and commended everybody he saw, monks, nuns, men and women disciples; speaking thus: 'I deeply revere you. Wherefore? Because you are walking in the bodhisattva way and are to become Buddhas.' That

monk did not devote himself to reading and reciting
the Sutras, but only to paying respect, so that when
he saw afar off a member of the four classes of disciples, he would specially go and pay respect to them,
commending them, saying: 'I dare not slight you,
because you are all to become Buddhas.' Amongst
the four classes, there were those who, irritated and
angry and low-minded, reviled and abused him
saying: 'Where does this ignorant bhikshu come from,
who takes it on himself to say, "I do not slight you,"
and who predicts us as destined to become Buddhas?
We need no such false predictions.' Thus, he passed
many years, constantly reviled but never irritated or
angry, always saying: 'You are to become Buddhas.'
Whenever he spoke thus, they beat him with clubs,
sticks, potsherds, or stones. But, while escaping to
a distance, he still cried aloud: 'I dare not slight you.
You are all to become Buddhas.' And because he
always spoke thus, the haughty monks, nuns, and
their disciples dubbed him: Never Despise.

"When this monk was drawing near his end, from
the sky he heard, and was perfectly able to receive and
retain, twenty thousand myriad kotis of verses of the
Law-Flower Sutra, which the Buddha, King of
Majestic Voice, had formerly preached. Whereupon
he obtained, as stated above, clearness and purity of
eye-organ, as also of the organs of ear, nose, tongue,
body, and thought. Having obtained the purity of
these six organs, he further prolonged his life for two
hundred myriad kotis of nayutas of years, and abundantly preached this Law-Flower Sutra to the people.

Then the haughty four orders of monks, nuns, and male and female disciples, who had slighted and contemned this man, and given him the name Never-Despise, seeing him possessed of great transcendent powers, of power of eloquent discourse, and power of excellent meditation, and having heard his preaching, believed in and followed him. This Bodhisattva again converted thousands, myriads, kotis of beings to Perfect Enlightenment."

Afterwards he preached the Sutra to countless Buddhas in different realms through infinite aeons. And who was this Bodhisattva Never-Despise? The Buddha says:

"He was I myself. If I, in my former lives, had not received and kept, read and recited this Sutra, and preached it to others, I should not have been able so soon to attain to Perfect Enlightenment. Because, under former Buddhas, I received and kept, read and recited this Sutra, and preached it to others, I so soon attained to Perfect Enlightenment."

"The Never-Despise of that time
Is really I myself.
The four groups of that time
Attached to external things

.   .   .   .   .

Are you of this assembly.
Age by age have I kept
This so wonderful a Sutra.
During kotis and kotis of kalpas

Of inconceivable extent,
Rare are the times that we heard
This Law-Flower Sutra preached.
During kotis and kotis of kalpas,
Inconceivable of extent,
Buddhas, World-honoured Ones,
But rarely preach this Sutra.
Therefore, let his followers,
After the Buddha's extinction,
On hearing such Sutra as this,
Conceive no doubt or perplexity.
But let them with single mind
Publish abroad this Sutra
And, age by age meeting Buddhas,
To Buddhahood will they speedily attain."

XXI

THE vast body of Bodhisattvas who sprang out of the earth, as recorded in Chapter XV, now fold their hands before the Buddha and, looking towards him, declare that they will preach this Sutra, in whatsoever worlds the Buddha, in any of his transformations, may exist and cease to exist.

By this declaration the World-honoured One is now moved to reveal his majestic divine power. In a miraculous way, attractive only to those who can see in it the symbolism intended, he showed the illuminating and far-reaching power of his organ of speech. In the presence of

"Manjuśri and the countless hundreds, thousands, myriads, kotis of Great Bodhisattvas, as well as of monks, nuns, male and female disciples, gods, dragons, yakshas, gandharvas, asuras, garudas, kinnaras, mahoragas, human and non-human beings, and so forth"—before all these beings, he "reveals his great divine power, by putting forth his broad and far-stretched tongue, till it reaches upward to the Brahma-world, every pore radiating the light of infinite, numberless colours, shining everywhere throughout each direction of the universe. Under the jewel-trees, the Buddhas, each seated on a Lion-throne, also in like manner put forth their broad far-stretched tongues, radiating infinite light. While Śakyamuni-Buddha, and the other Buddhas under

11. Yashada stretching out his arm to hold back the sun to enable King
Aśoka to build 84,000 stupas in one day

the jewel-trees, are thus revealing their divine powers, fully hundreds of thousands of years pass. After this they draw back their tongues, cough simultaneously, and snap their fingers in unison. These two sounds reach through every region of the Buddha-worlds, those worlds being shaken in every direction.

"In the midst of these worlds, all living beings . . . through the divine power of the Buddha, while in their world, see infinite, boundless, hundreds, thousands, myriads, kotis of Buddhas, seated on Lion-thrones under the jewel-trees; and see Sakyamuni-Buddha, together with the Tathagata Abundant-Treasures, seated on Lion-thrones in the midst of the Stupas; and also see infinite, boundless, hundreds, thousands, myriads, kotis of Great Bodhisattvas, and the four groups of disciples who reverently surround Sakyamuni-Buddha."

The gods, too, see and rejoice, crying "Namah! Sakyamuni-Buddha". Then from every quarter the gods from afar strew flowers, incense, garlands, and jewels, which form themselves "like gathering clouds, transforming into a jewelled canopy, covering the sky above the Buddhas".

"And upon this the worlds of all the universes are united without barrier as one Buddha-land."

Then the Buddha addresses Excellent-Conduct and the host of Bodhisattvas:

"The divine powers of Buddhas are so infinite and boundless that they are beyond thought and expression. Even if I, by these divine powers, through infinite, boundless, hundreds, thousands, myriads, kotis of numberless kalpas, for the sake of entailing them, were to declare the merits of this Sutra, I should still be unable to reach their end. Essentially speaking, all the laws belonging to Tathagata, all the sovereign, divine powers of Tathagata, all the mysterious, essential treasuries of Tathagata, and the most profound affairs of Tathagata, are proclaimed, displayed, revealed, and expounded in this Sutra. Therefore you should, after the extinction of the Tathagata, whole-heartedly receive and keep, read and recite, explain and copy, cultivate and practise it as taught. In whatever land, whether it be received and kept, read and recited, explained and copied, cultivated and practised as taught; whether in a place where a volume of the Sutra is kept, or in a temple, or in a grove, or under a tree, or in a monastery, or in a lay devotee's house, in a palace, or on a mountain, in a valley, or in the wilderness, in these places you must erect a stupa and make offerings. Wherefore? You should know that these spots are thrones of enlightenment. On these spots the Buddhas attain to Perfect Enlightenment: on these spots the Buddhas roll the Wheel of the Law; on these spots the Buddhas enter Parinirvana."

"He who is able to keep this Sutra
Is one who now and always beholds me,
And also Buddha Abundant Treasures

. . . . .

Just as the wind in the firmament
Never has impediment,

Just as the light of sun and moon
Is able to dispel the darkness,
So this man, walking in the world,
Can disperse the gloom of the living,
And cause numberless bodhisattvas
To abide in the One Great Vehicle."

XXII

ON this Śakyamuni Buddha arises from the Lion-throne in the sky, where he has been seated with the Buddha Abundant-Treasures, and by his supernatural power lays his right hand on the heads of the countless Great Bodhisattvas, saying:

"I, for incalculable hundreds, thousands, myriads, kotis of numberless kalpas have practised this rare law of Perfect Enlightenment. Now I entrust it to you. Do you with all your mind promulgate this Law, and make it increase and prosper far and wide."

Three times does he thus place his hand on their heads, and give them his final commission, before his entry into Nirvana. For

"the Tathagata is most benevolent and compassionate, not mean and grudging; he is able fearlessly to give the Buddha-Wisdom, the Tathagata-Wisdom, and the Self-Existent Wisdom to the living. The Tathagata is the great Lord of Giving to all living beings. Do you also follow and learn the Tathagata's example, ungrudgingly. If good sons or good daughters, in ages to come, believe in the Tathagata-wisdom, do you proclaim this Law-Flower Sutra to them that they may hear and know it, in order that they may obtain the Buddha-wisdom. If there be living beings who do not believe it, do you direct, teach, profit, and rejoice them with the other profound laws of the Tathagata. If you are able thus to act, then you will have repaid the grace of the Buddhas."

Thereupon they all, filled with joy, make obeisance, and cry three times with united voice, "We will do as the World-honoured One has commanded. Yes, World-honoured One! Have no anxiety."

"On this Śākyamuni Buddha causes the emanated Buddhas, who had come from all directions, each to return to his own land, saying: 'Buddhas! Peace be upon you. Let the Stupa of the Buddha Abundant-Treasures be restored as before'.

"As these words are spoken, the innumerable emanated Buddhas from every direction, who are seated on Lion-thrones under the jewel-trees, as well as the Buddha Abundant-Treasures, the host of infinite, numberless Bodhisattvas, Superior-Conduct and others, also the four groups of hearers, Śāriputra and others, and the worlds, gods, men, asuras and so on, hearing the words of the Buddha, all rejoice greatly."

XXIII

It is probable that with the preceding chapter the author ends his religious drama, as already has been mentioned in the Introduction, to which the reader is referred. The succeeding chapters add little to the apocalyptic conception but, whether originally part of the author's work or not, they have a value of their own as showing ideas current in Northern Buddhism early in our era.

In this chapter the starry sky seems to be represented by a Bodhisattva who may be described as King of the Star-Cluster—perhaps of Ursa Major. He asks the Buddha why the Bodhisattva Medicine-King, or King of Healing, wanders for countless aeons in suffering through the worlds. To him and the assembled host the Buddha replies that, of yore, there was a Buddha named Brilliance of Sun and Moon. Amongst the incalculable entities of his realm, "no women, no hells, no hungry ghosts, no animals, no titans, no disasters" found a place. While the gods discoursed celestial music this Buddha, who seems to represent the Light, preached the Law-Flower Sutra to a Bodhisattva called Beautiful. So full of rapture did Beautiful become, that he resolved to express his gratitude by the immolation of his beautiful body. Before so doing, he partook of all the fragrance of all the flowers for twelve hundred years. Then he anointed his body with costly unguents, wrapped himself in a celestial robe, bathed in perfumed oil, and by his transcendent will set fire to his body. The brightness illuminated all worlds, the Buddhas in which acclaimed his deed as "true zeal"; "the True Law Homage to the Tathagata"; "the supreme gift". His body continued to burn and illuminate the worlds for twelve hundred years, after which it came to an end.

Bodhisattva Beautiful was reborn by transformation in the domain of the same Buddha, into the home of King Virtue. He forthwith informed the King, that he had obtained the spell which enabled him to interpret the utterances of all the living; moreover that he had heard the Law-Flower Sutra in countless verses. He must needs pay his Buddha a visit of homage, and at once, seated on a lofty tower, he rose into the sky.

The Buddha thereupon announced to him his own departure: "My good son! The time of my Nirvana has come. The time of my extinction has arrived. You may arrange my bed. To-night I shall enter Parinirvana". He committed his Law, his disciples, his realm, his relics to Beautiful, and the same night passed away. Beautiful mourned him, deeply moved and distressed; then on a costly sandal-wood pyre burnt the body, collected the relics, made eighty-four thousand precious urns and erected the same number of Stupas with richest adornment.

Still unsatisfied with his devotion, he further set fire to his own arms, which burnt for seventy-two thousand years, bringing vast hosts of people to seek Perfect Enlightenment. All mourned and lamented over his burnt-off arms and deformed body. To comfort them and reveal his divine power, he restored his arms as before. The Milky Way, its disappearance and return, is suggestive of the lost arms and their reappearance.

Śakyamuni is now made to say, that Beautiful has become the present Bodhisattva, the King of Healing. Such has been his example of self-immolation that, "if any one with mind set on attaining Perfect Enlightenment is able to burn a finger of his own hand, or even a toe of his foot, in homage to a Buddha's stupa, he surpasses any other who pays homage with domain, cities, wives, and children."

This Sutra is as vast as is the ocean to the streams and rivers; as is Mount Sumeru, the great mountain of the world, to the other hills; as are the sun and moon to the stars; and, in short, "just as the Buddha is king of the laws (or of all things) so is it with this Sutra: it is King among the Sutras."

"Just as a clear and cool pool is able to satisfy all those who are thirsty, and as is the condition of the cold who obtain a fire, the naked who find clothing, a caravan of merchants who find a leader, children who find a mother, one who at a ferry finds a boat, a sick man who finds a doctor, one in the darkness who obtains a lamp, a poor man who finds a jewel, a people who find a king, merchant-venturers who gain the sea, and a torch which dispels the darkness, so is it also in regard to this Law-Flower Sutra. It is able to deliver

238

the living from all sufferings and diseases, and is able to unloose the bonds of mortal life.

"If any one, hearing this Law-Flower Sutra, either himself copies, or causes others to copy it, the limits of the sum of merit to be obtained cannot be calculated even by Buddha-wisdom. If any one copies this Sutra and pays homage to it with flowers, scents, necklaces, incense, sandal-powder, unguents, flags, canopies, garments, and various kinds of lamps: ghee lamps, oil lamps, lamps of scented oil, lamps of Campaka oil, lamps of Samana oil, lamps of Patala oil, lamps of Varshika oil, and lamps of Navamalika oil, the merit to be obtained by him is equally inestimable.

"King of the Star-Cluster! If there be any one who hears this chapter of the Former Act of the Bodhisattva King of Healing, he will also obtain infinite and boundless merits. If there be any woman who hears this chapter of the Former Deed of the Bodhisattva King of Healing, and is able to receive and keep it, she, after the end of her present woman's body, will not again receive it. If, after the extinction of the Buddha, in the last five hundred years, there be any woman who hears this Sutra and acts according to its teaching; at the close of this life she will go to the Happy World where Amitayus Buddha dwells, encompassed by his host of great Bodhisattvas, and will there be born in the midst of a lotus-flower upon a jewelled throne. Never again will he (the transformed woman) be harassed by desire, nor be harassed by anger and foolishness, nor again be harassed by pride, envy, or uncleanness, but will attain to transcendent powers and the Assurance of No-rebirth; and having obtained this assurance, the organ of the eye will be serene, by which serene organ of the eye he will see seven million two thousand kotis of nayutas of Buddha-Tathagatas, equal to the sands of the Ganges river, when these Buddhas from afar will unite in lauding him, saying: 'Excellent, excellent! Good son! You have been able to receive and keep, read and recite, and ponder on this Sutra of the Law of Śakyamuni Buddha and to expound it to others. The blessed merit you have obtained is infinite and boundless; fire cannot burn it, water cannot wash it away. Your merit is beyond the power of a thousand Buddhas to explain. You have now been able to destroy the Mara-marauders, to overthrow the hostile forces of mortality, and to crush out all other enemies. Good son! Hundreds of thousands of Buddhas, with their transcendent powers, together guard and protect you. Among the gods and men of all worlds none can equal you, except the Tathagata."

Any one who receives this chapter will "ever breathe out the fragrance of the blue lotus flower, and out of the pores of his body will come fragrance of sandal-wood". Such is the symbolic way of presenting the fragrant life. "If a man be sick, on hearing this Sutra his sickness will instantly disappear, and he will neither grow old nor die." The implication may be that the man is spirit and therefore cannot grow old and die.

Finally the Tathagata Abundant Treasures, from the Celestial Shrine, praises the King of the Star-cluster for having been able to obtain from Sakyamuni Buddha "such things as these, and thereby infinitely benefit all the living".

XXIV

A DOUBLE ray issues from Buddha's brow and illuminates eastwards a hundred and eight myriad kotis of nayutas of Buddha worlds, as the sands of Ganges in number. Beyond these is revealed a world named Adorned-with-Pure-Radiance, whose king is King Wisdom of the Pure-Flower Constellation. Among his vast host of Bodhisattvas is one called Wonder-Sound. The symbolism is that of the thunder and the lightning. He had served numberless Buddhas and attained to innumerable samadhis, giving him insight into Causelessness, Sun-revolution, Interpretation of all Sounds, and many others whose names are given.

Wonder-Sound now begs permission to leave his far distant world and visit Śakyamuni in this world. His Buddha-King gives him permission, but warns him not to expect it to be like his own beautiful world. The world he proposes to visit is a poor, rough place, full of hills and valleys;

"full of earth, stones, mounds, and filth; the body of the Buddha is short and small, and all the bodhisattvas are small of stature, whereas your body is forty-two thousand yojanas high and my body sixty-eight hundred thousand yojanas. Your body is of the finest order, blest with hundreds, thousands, myriads of felicities, and of a wonderful brightness. Therefore on resorting there, do not look lightly on that domain, nor conceive a low opinion of the Buddha, nor of the bodhisattvas, nor of their country.

"The Bodhisattva Wonder-Sound replied to the Buddha: 'World-honoured One! That I now go to visit the Saha-world is all due to the Tathagata's power, the Tathagata's magic power of travelling, and the Tathagata's adornment of merit and wisdom.'

"Thereupon the Bodhisattva Wonder-Sound, without rising from his seat and without stirring his body, entered into samadhi. By the power of his samadhi, on the Mount Gridhrakuta, not far distant from the Law-seat, there appeared in transformation eighty-four thousand precious lotus-flowers with stalks of gold, leaves of silver, and ruby-flowers with stamens of diamonds."

Manjuśri questions Śakyamuni as to the meaning of this auspicious sign, to which the reply is given that the great Bodhisattva Wonder-Sound has sent it to announce his intention to come and hear the Lotus Sutra, along with his train of disciples, eight-four thousand in number. Manjuśri again questions the Buddha: "World-honoured One! What roots of goodness has that Bodhisattva planted, what merits has he cultivated, that he should be able to have such transcendent power?" In answer, the Buddha Abundant Treasures signs to Wonder-Sound to come in person with his train. Thereupon Wonder-Sound sets out to pass over all the vast number of intervening domains, each of which is shaken by his passage, while lotus flowers rain everywhere, and celestial instruments send forth without hands divine music. His eyes are like broad big leaves of the blue lotus, his brow the glory of myriads of moons, his body is radiant like pure gold. He is of glowing majesty.

Arriving he alights from his seven-jewelled tower and takes a priceless necklace to offer to Śākyamuni Buddha, making obeisance at his feet and saying,

"World-honoured One! The Buddha 'King Wisdom of the Pure-Flower-Constellation' inquires after the World-honoured One thus: 'Hast thou few ailments and few harassments? Art thou at ease and in comfort? Are thy four component parts in harmony? Are thy worldly affairs tolerable? Are thy creatures easy to save—not over-covetous, angry, foolish, envious, arrogant; never unfilial to parents or irreverent to their teachers? Have they perverted views, or are they of good mind and restrained in their five passions? World-honoured One! Are thy creatures able to overcome the Māra-enemies? Does the Tathāgata Abundant-Treasures, so long extinct, still abide in the Stūpa of the Precious Seven, and come to listen to the Law?' King Wisdom also inquires of the Tathāgata Abundant-Treasures: 'Art thou at ease and of few harassments? Wilt thou be content to remain long?' World-honoured One! We now would see the bodily form of the Buddha Abundant-Treasures. Be pleased, World-honoured One, to show and let us see him."

"Then says Śākyamuni Buddha to the Buddha Abundant-Treasures: 'This Bodhisattva Wonder-Sound desires an interview.' Instantly the Buddha

Abundant-Treasures addresses Wonder-Sound: 'Excellent, excellent! That you have been able to come here to pay homage to Śakyamuni Buddha, to hear the Law-Flower Sutra, and to see Manjuśri and the others'."

Śakyamuni here tells an inquiring disciple, that Wonder-Sound had formerly paid homage to the King of Cloud-thundering, and obtained great powers. He tells them that they see here but one of his manifold bodies. To preach the Lotus Sutra he appears in many forms.

"Sometimes he appears as Brahma, or appears as Sakra, or appears as Isvara, as Mahesvara, or as a deva-general, or as the deva-king Vaisravana, or as a Holy Wheel-rolling King, or as one of the ordinary kings, or as an elder, as a citizen, or a minister; or appears as a Brahman; or appears as a monk, a nun, a disciple male or female; or appears as the wife of an elder or a citizen, or as the wife of a minister, or of a Brahman, or as a youth or maiden; or appears as a god, dragon, yaksha, gandharva, asura, garuda, kinnara, mahoraga, man, or a non-human being, and so on: and preaches this Sutra. He is able to rescue whatever beings are in the hells, or hungry ghosts, animals and all in distress. Even in the inner courts of a king, transforming himself into a woman, he preaches this Sutra."

His transformations accord with what may be expedient. To those he must save in the form of a Hinayana teacher, he appears in that form to preach the Law; to those he must save in the form of a Bodhisattva, or a Buddha, he appears in that form; even to those he must save by his extinction, he reveals himself as extinct. These mighty powers he attained through the samadhi-meditation "Revelation-of-all-powers".

When Wonder-Sound has paid his homage to Sakyamuni and the Buddha Abundant-Treasures, he returns to his own land accompanied by his disciples, and attended with phenomena like those which announced his progress hither.

And while the chapter on the going and coming of the Bodhisattva Wonder-Sound was preached, forty-two thousand heavenly sons attained to the Assurance of No-Rebirth, and the Bodhisattva Flower-Virtue attained to the samadhi termed Law-Flower.

XXV

From his seat arises the Bodhisattva Infinite-Thought who, baring his right shoulder and folding his hands, asks the Buddha why the Bodhisattva Kwan-shi-yin is thus named, Regarder of the Cries of the World. The Buddha replies:

"If there be any who hold fast to the name of that Bodhisattva, Regarder-of-the-Cries-of-the-World, though they fall into a great fire, the fire will not be able to burn them, by virtue of the august supernatural power of that Bodhisattva. If any, carried away by a flood, call upon (his) name, they will immediately reach the shallows. If there be hundreds, thousands, myriads, kotis of beings, who in search of gold, silver, lapis lazuli, moon-stones, agate, coral, amber, pearls, and other treasures, go out on the ocean, and if a black gale blows their ships adrift upon the land of the Rakshasa-demons, and if amongst them there be even a single person who calls the name of the Bodhisattva Regarder-of-the-Cries-of-the-World, all those people will be delivered from the woes of the Rakshasas. It is for this cause that he is named Regarder-of-the-Cries-of-the-World.

"Or if any one cries who is in deadly peril by the sword, the sword will be snapped asunder. If wicked demons attack, the one who cries will become invisible to them. Whether guilty or innocent, if he cry, though loaded with manacles, fetters, cangues or chains, all will be broken and he will be set free. A train of jewel-merchants, passing along a road infested with robbers, have but to cry with one voice and they will be protected. Those possessed by carnal passions, anger, or infatuation have but to remember and revere this Bodhisattva and they will be set free. If a woman desires a son, worships and pays homage, she will bear a son, virtuous and wise; or if a daughter, then of good demeanour and looks.

"The merit attained by worship of other Bodhisattvas, in number as sands of sixty-two kotis of Ganges, just equals the merit of him who but for one moment worships the Regarder-of-the-Cries-of-the-World."

This Bodhisattva appears to all according to their need. If needed as a Hinayana teacher, he appears as such; if as Brahma, or Indra, or Isvara, or a deva, a king, an elder, a citizen, an official, a brahman, a monk, nun, or male or female disciple, then he appears as such. If needed in the form of a wife of an elder, citizen, official or brahman, he appears as such; or if as a youth or maiden, he appears as such. If needed as a god, or a demon, he so appears. This is given in lengthy detail.

Kwan-yin, or Kwan-non, is to-day represented as a female Bodhisattva and by Europeans styled the Goddess of Mercy. She is addressed as "Most Merciful, Most Pitiful". In reality Kwan-yin is above sex, and may be represented as male or female. Kwan-yin, this Sutra tells us, is the great Bestower of Fearlessness, relieving the fear of those who are in anxiety or distress.

12. Kuan-yin breaking the executioner's sword

From an A. D. 1681 facsimile of an A. D. 1331 edition of the illustrated
Kuan-yin chapter of the Lotus Sutra

"Listen to the deeds of the Cry-Regarder,
Who well responds to every quarter;
Vast is his vow as deep the sea,
Age-long, and inconceivable.

.   .   .   .   .

Who hears his name and looks to him,
Unremittingly remembering him,
Will end the sorrows of existence.
Even though men with ill intent
Cast him into a burning pit,
Let him think of the Cry-Regarder
The very fire-pit becomes a pool;
Or, driven along a mighty ocean
In peril dire of dragons and demons,
Let him think of the Cry-Regarder
And ne'er will waves him overwhelm;
Or if, from lofty peak of Sumeru,
They should hurl him headlong down,
Let him think of the Cry-Regarder
And firm as the sun he is held in the sky.

.   .   .   .   .

If by incantations or poison
Any one seeks to hurt his body,
And he thinks of the Cry-Regarder,
All these ills revert to their author.

.   .   .   .   .

If, encompassed by evil beasts,
Sharp of tusk or cruel of claw,
He should think of the Cry-Regarder,

They will flee in every direction;
Or there be boas, vipers and scorpions,
Breathing poison as fire-flame scorching,
If he thinks of the Cry-Regarder,
Instantly they each will vanish.

.   .   .   .   .

Every evil state of existence,
Hells and ghosts and animals,
Sorrows of birth, age, disease, death,
All will thus be ended for him.
True Regard, serene Regard,
Far-reaching, wise Regard,
Regard of pity, Regard compassionate,
Ever longed for, ever looked for
In radiance ever pure and serene!
Wisdom's sun, destroying darkness,
Subduer of woes, of storm, of fire,
Illuminator of the world!
Law of pity, thunder quivering,
Compassion wondrous as a great cloud,
Pouring spiritual rain like nectar,
Quenching all the flames of distress!

.   .   .   .   .

Voice of the Regarder, wondrous Voice,
Voice of the rolling tide, Brahma-voice,
Voice all world-surpassing,
Ever to be cherished in mind
With never a doubting thought.
World's Cry-Regarder, pure and holy,
In pain, distress, in death or woe,

Potent as a sure reliance,
Perfect in every virtuous merit,
All-beholding with eyes of pity,
Boundless ocean-store of blessings!
Prostrate, let us make obeisance."

.   .   .   .   .

"While the Buddha preached this chapter of the All-sided One, the eighty-four thousand living beings in the assembly set their minds on Perfect Enlightenment, with which nothing can compare."

XXVI

THE Bodhisattva, King of Healing, is now represented offering spells to guard and protect the
preachers of the Lotus Sutra. One such spell
begins:

"Anye manye mane mamane citte carite same sami-
tavi sante mukte muktanesame avishame sama same
jaye khshaye akshaye akshine sante samite dharani
alokabhashe-pratyavekshani nidhini abhyantarani-
vishte . . ." and so on.

This is a spell, he says, which has been used by
Buddhas numerous as the sands of sixty-two kotis
of Ganges, and if any one does violence to the
teachers of the Lotus Sutra, they will be doing
violence to all these Buddhas. Sakyamuni extolls
the King of Healing for his wonderful spell.

Another Bodhisattva, Courageous-Giver, then
offers another spell against all demons, com-
mencing, "Jvale mahajvale ukke tukku mukku
ude . . ." &c.

A deva-king also offers a spell potent in his
realm: "Atte tatte natte vanatte anade nadi kumadi
avaha . . ." Another deva-king offers yet another.

Rakshasas, that is non-human "furies" or
witches, named Binder, Unbinder, Crooked-teeth,
Coloured-teeth, Black-teeth, Dishevelled-locks, In-
satiable, Skull- or Necklace-holder, Kunti and
Spirit-snatcher: these ten creatures, together with

13. The Mara-king offering his protective spells to the Buddha

the Mother-of-Demon-Sons, with her children and followers, now approach, offering their spells.

"If any spy for the shortcomings of these teachers of the Law, we will prevent their obtaining their wish." The spell they give is:

"Iti me, iti me, iti me, iti me, iti me; ni me, ni me, ni me, ni me, ni me; ruhe, ruhe, ruhe, ruhe, ruhe; stuhe, stuhe, stuhe, stuhe, stuhe, svaha.

"Let troubles come on our heads rather than on theirs."

Neither yakshas nor hungry ghosts, nor the long list of malevolent creatures, whose names are given, nor fevers of any kind shall cause the preacher of the Lotus Sutra distress. They add:

"Whoever dares defy our spell
And harass any preacher,
May his head be split in seven,
Like unto an arjaka sprout.
His doom be that of a parricide,
Or of a swindling oil-presser,
Or of a cheat with measure and weight,
Or of Devadatta the first schismatic.
He who dares offend these Preachers,
Such shall be his certain doom."

The Buddha replies to these witches, that great shall be their reward if they protect those who only keep the name of this Sutra in mind; how much greater those who pay homage to it

"with flowers, incense, necklaces, sandal-powder,

perfumes, incense, flages, canopies, and music; burning various kinds of lamps—ghee lamps, oil lamps, lamps of scented oil, lamps of oil of Campaka-flowers, lamps of oil of Varshika-flowers, and lamps of oil of Udumbara-flowers; such hundreds thousands kinds of offerings as these. Kunti! You and your followers ought to protect such teachers of the Law."

"While this chapter of Dharanis was preached, thirty-eight thousand people attained to the Assurance of No-Rebirth."

XXVII

THE Buddha now tells the story of King Resplendent. Of yore, infinite aeons ago, there was a Buddha called Thunder-Voice, who was the Star-King Wisdom. His realm was named Radiantly-Adorned, and his epoch Joyful-Sight.

In his domain was a king called Resplendent, whose wife was Pure Virtue, and his two sons, one Pure Treasury, the other Pure Eyes. The two sons had attained to great supernatural powers, blessedness and wisdom, by methods of self-cultivation and concentration, the names of which are given; and by "benevolence, compassion, joy, indifference and the thirty-seven kinds of aids to the Way".

Then the Buddha Thunder-Voice decided to guide King Resplendent into the higher truth, by preaching to him this Lotus Sutra. The two sons, becoming aware of this intention, implored their mother to lead them to hear the Sutra. The mother sighed that the father believed in and was deeply attached to heretical doctrine, but sent her two sons to urge him to accompany them. The two sons, putting their religion first, protested that, "though born in this home of heretical views", they were really the sons of Buddha. Again the mother urged them: "You should have sympathy with your father, and reveal to him some of your supernatural powers so that, seeing them, his mind may be enlightened, and he may perhaps grant that we all go to the Buddha."

On this the sons went to the king and, in order to convince him, displayed their marvellous powers, rising into the sky, walking, sitting, standing and lying there. They expanded themselves till they filled the whole sky, or shrunk themselves to minute size; they vanished from the sky and appeared upon earth; they entered the earth as if it were water, and walked on water as on the earth. Thus they convinced their father and brought him to faith and discernment. Demanding to be told who was their teacher, he was informed it was Thunder-Voice, Star-King of Wisdom.

"I also would now like to see your Master," said the King; "we will all go together."

The sons reported to their mother and begged for permission to leave home and become followers of the Buddha.

"I grant you permission to leave home," she graciously said; "for it is a rare event in the world to meet a Buddha."

They besought both father and mother to go and pay homage to the Buddha, for, said they, a Buddha is as rare an event as is the flower of the tree that blossoms but once in its life-time; or as "a one-eyed tortoise spying the sun through a hole in a floating log". "But we, richly blessed through a former lot, now may meet the Buddha in this life."

Then the eighty-four thousand court ladies of King Resplendent also became capable of receiving the Lotus Sutra.

"Thereupon King Resplendent, accompanied by his ministers and retinue, Queen Pure Virtue with her court ladies and retinue, and the two Princes, together with forty-two thousand of their people, set out to visit the Buddha."

After prostrating themselves, they made procession around the Buddha three times and stood on either side.

"Then that Buddha preached to the king, showing, teaching, profiting, rejoicing him, so that the king was greatly delighted. King Resplendent and his Queen unloosed the necklaces of pearls worth hundreds and thousands, from their necks, and threw them upon the Buddha, and these in the sky were transformed into a four-column jewel-tower; on the tower was a large jewelled couch spread with hundreds, thousands, myriads of celestial coverings, on which sat the Buddha cross-legged, emitting a great ray of light. Whereupon King Resplendent reflected thus: 'Rare, dignified, extraordinary is the Buddha's body, perfect in its supreme refined colouring'."

"The king at once made over his domain to his younger brother; while he, together with his queen, two sons and their retinue, forsook his home, and followed the Way under the rule of that Buddha. Having forsaken his home, during eighty-four thousand years the king was ever diligent and zealous in observing the Wonderful Law-Flower Sutra, and after these years had passed, attained to the samadhi Adorned-with-all-pure-Merits.

Rising in the sky King Resplendent gave the praise for his enlightenment to his two sons, who had turned his mind from heresy to Buddha Truth. "These two sons are indeed my good friends, for desiring to develop the good roots planted by me in my former lives, they came and were born in my home." In other words, the good seed the King had sown in former lives attracted these two spirits to be born in his home, to aid him in reaping the fruit. The implication is that no man has sons of his own. He may beget their bodies, but the real sons are souls re-born into his home.

"So it is, so it is," the Buddha replied, "It is as you say. Any good son or good daughter, by planting roots of goodness, will in every generation obtain good friends, which good friends will be able to do Buddha-deeds, showing, teaching, profiting and rejoicing him, and causing him to enter into Perfect Enlightenment. Know, Great King! A good friend is the great cause whereby men are converted and led to see the Buddha and aroused to Perfect Enlightenment. Great King! Do you see these two sons? These two sons have already paid homage to Buddhas sixty-five times the hundreds, thousands, myriads, kotis nayutas of the sands of a Ganges, waiting upon and revering them; and among those Buddhas have received and kept the Law-Flower Sutra, compassionating the living in their false views, and establishing them in right views."

"King Resplendent thereupon descended from the sky and said to the Buddha:

'World-honoured One! Rare indeed is the sight of the Tathagata; by his merits and wisdom the prominence on his head shines brilliantly; his eyes are wide-open and deep blue; the tuft between his eyebrows is white as the pearly moon; his teeth are wide, even, close and ever shining; his lips are red and beautiful as bimba-fruit.'

"When King Resplendent had thus extolled the many merits of that Buddha—countless hundreds, thousands, myriads, kotis of them—with all his mind he folded his hands before the Tathagata and again addressed that Buddha saying: 'Unprecedented is the World-honoured One. The Tathagata's teaching is perfect in its inconceivable and wonderful merits. The moral precepts which he promulgates are comforting and quickening. From this day onward I will not again follow my own mind, nor beget false views, nor a haughty, angry or any other sinful mind.' Having uttered these words, he did reverence to the Buddha and went forth."

Sakyamuni now declares that King Resplendent and his queen are re-incarnated in the persons of two Bodhisattvas present, and that the two princes are now the Bodhisattvas King of Healing and Lord of Healing.

"While the Buddha preached this chapter, eighty-four thousand people departed from impurity, separated themselves from uncleanness, and acquired pure spiritual eyes in regard to spiritual things."

XXVIII

THEN from the East comes the Bodhisattva, Universal-Virtue, with his unlimited, infinite, incalculable host. Countless realms are shaken by his passage, while jewel-lotuses rain down upon them, and numberless celestial instruments pour forth their exquisite music. He, too, has heard that the Lotus Sutra is being preached and has brought his host of Bodhisattvas to hear it.

The Buddha responds to him, announcing what may be considered as the equivalent in Mahayana for the Four Noble Truths of the Hinayana.

"If any good son or daughter acquires the four following requisites, such a one will possess this Law-Flower Sutra after the extinction of the Tathagata:

"First, place himself under the care of Buddhas:
Second, plant the roots of virtue:
Third, enter into correct concentration (or meditation):
Fourth, seek the salvation of all the living.

Any good son or good daughter, who attains to these four requisites, will assuredly possess this Sutra after the extinction of the Tathagata."

Thereupon the Bodhisattva Universal-Virtue, whose title may be taken to indicate the moral basis and catholicism of Mahayana, promises to protect those who keep this Truth, and to give ease of mind and freedom from the affliction of Mara, Mara-sons, Mara-daughters, Mara-people, Mara-satellites, yakshas and so on.

"Wherever such a one walks or stands, reading and reciting this Sutra, I will at once mount the royal six-tusked white elephant and, with a host of great Bodhisattvas, go to that place and, revealing myself, will serve and protect him, comforting his mind; also thereby serving the Law-Flower Sutra. Wherever such a one sits, pondering over this Sutra, I will at once again mount the royal white elephant and show myself to him. If such a one forgets, be it but a single word or verse of the Law-Flower Sutra, I will teach him it, read and recite it with him, and again cause him to master it. Thereupon he who receives and keeps, reads and recites the Law-Flower Sutra, on seeing me will greatly rejoice and renew his zeal. Through seeing me, he will at once attain to the samadhis and the dharanis."

Wherever the followers of this Sutra meet together for three sevenfold days, then Universal Truth declares:

"I will mount my six-tusked white elephant, and accompanied by countless Bodhisattvas, appear before those people in the form the living delight to see, and preach to them, revealing, instructing, bene-fitting and rejoicing them. Moreover I will give them spells, so that no human or non-human beings can injure them, nor any woman beguile them."

Such is the promise of the spiritual presence, power, and aid of Universal Virtue.

Those who keep, read, remember, apprehend, and practise the Sutra as preached are assured that they are "doing the works of Universal-Virtue, have deeply planted roots of goodness under numberless, countless Buddhas, and that their heads will be caressed by the hands of the Tathagatas". If they merely copy this Sutra, they will be reborn in a heaven, where they will be welcomed with music by eighty-four thousand nymphs, and they, wearing jewelled crowns, will dwell among those nymphs, joyful and delighted. If such be the reward of a mere copyist, how much greater will be the reward of him who reads, remembers, and practises it. To him

"the hands of a thousand Buddhas will be offered, that he may fear not, neither fall into any evil destiny, but go straight to Maitreya's heaven, where are hosts of Great Bodhisattvas and hundreds, thousands, myriads, kotis of nymph-followers; amongst these will he be re-born."

"Therefore," says Universal-Virtue, "the wise should with all their minds themselves copy it, or cause others to copy it, receive and keep, read and recite, rightly remember, and practise it as preached. World-honoured One! I now by my supernatural power will guard and protect this Sutra so that, after the extinction of the Tathagata, it may spread abroad without cease in the world."

"Then Sakyamuni Buddha extolls him, saying: 'It

is well, it is well, Universal Virtue, that you are able to protect and assist this Sutra, and bring happiness and weal to the living in so many places. You have already attained to inconceivable merits and profound benevolence and compassion. From a long distant past have you aspired to Perfect Enlightenment, and been able to make this supernatural vow to guard and protect this Sutra. And I, by supernatural power, will guard and protect those who are able to receive and keep the name of the Bodhisattva Universal-Virtue.

"Universal-Virtue! If there be any who receive and keep, read and recite, rightly remember, practise and copy this Law-Flower Sutra, know that such are attending on Sakyamuni Buddha, as if they were hearing this Sutra direct from the Buddha's mouth; know that such are paying homage to Sakyamuni Buddha; know that the Buddha is praising them, 'Well done!' Know that the heads of such are being caressed by the hands of Sakyamuni Buddha. Know that such are covered by the robe of Sakyamuni Buddha. Such as these will not again be eager for worldly pleasure, nor be fond of heretical scriptures and writings; nor ever again take pleasure in intimacy with worldly men, or with evil persons, whether butchers, or herders of boars, sheep, fowls, and dogs, or hunters, and panderers. But such as these will be right-minded, have correct aims and be auspicious. Such will not be harassed by the Three Poisons, nor be harassed by envy, pride, haughtiness, and arrogance; such will be content with few desires, and able to do the works of Universal-Virtue.

"Universal-Virtue! After the extinction of the Tathagata, in the latter five hundred years (of decadence), if any one sees one who receives and keeps, reads and recites the Law-Flower Sutra, he must reflect thus: 'This man will ere long go to the wisdom-plot, destroy the host of Mara, attain to Perfect Enlightenment, and rolling onward the Law-wheel, beating the Law-drum, blowing the Law-conch, and pouring the rain of the Law, will sit on the lion-throne of the Law amid a great assembly of gods and men.'

"Universal-Virtue! Whoever in future ages receive and keep, read and recite this Sutra, such persons will no longer be greedily attached to clothes, bedding, drink, food, and things for the support of life; whatever they wish will never be in vain, and in the present life they will obtain their blessed reward. Suppose any one slights and slanders them, saying: 'You are only mad men, pursuing this course in vain, with never a thing to be gained'—the doom for such sin as this is blindness, generation after generation. If any one makes offerings to and praises them, he will obtain visible reward in the present world. Again, if any one sees those who receive and keep this Sutra, and proclaims their errors and sins, whether true or false, such a one in the present life will be smitten with leprosy. If he ridicules them, generation after generation his teeth will be sparse and missing, his lips vile, his nose flat, his hands and feet contorted, his eyes asquint, his body stinking and filthy with evil scabs and bloody pus, he will be dropsical and short of breath, and have every evil disease. Therefore,

Universal-Virtue, if one sees those who receive and keep this Sutra, he should stand up and greet them from afar, just as if he were paying reverence to the Buddha."

"While the chapter of the Encouragement of the Bodhisattva Universal-Virtue was being preached, innumerable, incalculable Bodhisattvas, equal to the sands of Ganges, attained to the dharani of the Hundreds, Thousands, Myriads, Kotis of Progress, and Bodhisattvas equal to the atoms of a Three-Thousand-Great-Thousandfold World became perfect in the Way of Enlightenment.

"When the Buddha preached this Sutra, Universal-Virtue and the other Bodhisattvas, Sariputra and the other sravakas, and the gods, dragons, human and non-human beings, and all others in the great assembly, greatly rejoiced together, and taking possession of the Buddha's words, made salutation to him and withdrew."

Amitabha, p. 45, *ad fin*. Though Amitabha does not appear under this name, he is cursorily mentioned as Amitayus.

GLOSSARY

Ajita, idem Maitreya, *q. v.*

Amitābha, Amitāyus, or *Amita.* Infinite light and infinite life, possibly a Persian concept adapted by Mahāyānists. It is in this Sūtra that he first has mention. He is the most popular Buddha in the Far East, and to Sukhavatī, his Paradise, or Pure-land, where also Kuan-yin dwells, it is the prayer of most devotees to go.

Āṇanda, p. 146.

Anātman. Without a permanent personality, or soul.

Anuttara-samyak-sambōdhi. Unsurpassed perfect wisdom.

Araṇya. Hermitage.

Arhat, Arhān, in Chinese 'Lo-han'. One who has attained to spiritual ārya or saintship; one who strives after it; a higher class of Buddhist disciple.

Arjaka. Symplocos Racemosa; but it may be Marjaka which is said to split into seven pieces when cut down.

Asaṃkhyēya. Beyond number, countless, numberless; by some explained as 1 followed by 17 ciphers, by others as by 97 ciphers, by others as a world period of 1,344,000,000 years.

Asita, p. 20.

Aśōka. The first great royal patron of Buddhism in the third century B.C.; *see* p. 6.

Asuras. Titans, powerful rivals of the gods; *see* Nāga.

Avalōkiteśvara. Regarder of cries, Kuan-yin. The original form is uncertain.

Avīci. Unintermitted reincarnation in the last of the eight hot hells.

Avinivartanīyaḥ. Never retrograding, or returning to mortality.

Bhikshu, Bhikshuṇī. Mendicants, monks, nuns.

Bōdhi. Enlightenment; awake, aware, enlightened.

Bōdhisattva. A disciple who has become enlightened and freed from the miseries of mortality; also an angelic being ready for final buddhahood, who remains in a lower state to save others; *see* Mahāsattva.

Bōdhisattva-Mahāsattva. See Mahāsattva.

Brahmā. The first person in the Brahminical trinity. By Buddhists he is considered as subject to mortality, and therefore inferior to one who has attained to Bōdhi. In this Sūtra he is mentioned as the 'Father of all the living', perhaps as Dēva of the present world.

Brāhmaṇas. Brahmins, i.e. those of the highest caste.

Buddha. The enlightened; awake, aware.

267

Dēva. The gods of Brahminism; gods in general; they are all subject to metempsychosis.

Dēvadatta, p. 20.

Dhāraṇī. Magic formula, spell, incantation.

Dharmagupta, p. 7.

Dharmaraksha, p. 7.

Dhuta. Discipline.

Gandharva. Beings superior to men, able to smell incense and make music; *see* Nāga.

Garuḍa. Winged spirits resembling powerful birds able to fight Nāgas, *q. v.*

Gayā. An ancient city of Magadha, where Śākyamuni lived for seven years before attaining his enlightenment; pp. 197, 200.

Gṛidhrakūṭa. The Vulture Peak, p. 13.

Hīnayāna. Small conveyance, or vehicle; whereby the few are saved by works.

Indra. One of the most ancient gods of Brahminism, now protector of Buddhism, though considered inferior to a Buddha. His symbol is the vajra.

Īśvara. A sovereign (in his own right), *see* Maheśvara.

Jñānāgupta, p. 7.

Kalaviṅka. A fabulous bird of melodious song; p. 220.

Kalpa. There are many kinds, but the general meaning is an aeon or age.

Kanishka. See p. 6.

Karma. Deed, conduct, moral action; used also in the sense of character as the resultant of moral thought and action. *See* p. 44.

Kāśyapa. See Mahā-Kāśyapa.

Kinnara. Supernatural beings usually represented with horses' heads; the musicians of Kuvera, or Pluto; *see* Nāga.

Kōṭī. A figure varying from 100,000 to 10,000,000,000.

Kshatriyas. The second caste, of kings and warriors, from which Buddhas come.

Kumārajīva. See p. 7.

Kumbhāṇḍa. Monstrously deformed demons.

Kuntī. Name of a demoness.

Mahā-Kāśyapa. One of the principal disciples of the Buddha.

Mahāsattva. Great being. Bōdhisattvas superior to all beings except Buddhas, and who are saviours of all creatures.

Mahāyāna. Great vehicle; by which all are saved through faith.

Mahā-Kātyāyana. One of the four oldest disciples; p. 129.

Mahā-Māudgalyāyana. One of the four oldest disciples; p. 129.

Mahēśvara. King of dēvas. Śiva.

Mahōraga. Boa-demons; large bellied demons; *see* Nāga.

Māitrēya. The next Buddha, the Messiah of the Buddhists. Also called Ajita.

Mañjuśrī. An imaginary Bōdhisattva, the apotheosis of transcendental wisdom.

Māra. The murderer or enemy of goodness; the devil.

Nāga. Snake, boa, dragon, monster. The eight classes beyond the human stage are Dēvas, Nāgas, Rakshas, Gandharvas, Asuras, Garuḍas, Kinnaras, Mahōragas.

Namo, or *Namaḥ.* A formula of adoration, like Ave.

Nayuta. Some say a hundred thousand millions.

Nirvāṇa. Extinction, but whether of existence, or of reincarnation, or of all impurity, is much debated.

Pāramitās. The (six) virtues which ferry over the saṃsāra stream to nirvāna—renunciation, purity, endurance, advance, concentrated meditation, wisdom.

Parinirvāṇa. Final extinction, *see* Nirvāṇa.

Pratyēkabuddha. An individualist who saves himself but does not save others; an ascetic.

Puṇḍarīka. The great, or white lotus.

Rāhula. Son of the Buddha, born before the latter left home.

Rakshas. Demons who devour men, the retinue of Vāiśravana; *see* Nāga.

Saddharma. Good Law, True Law, somewhat similar to 'Gospel'. In Chinese it is translated by Miao Fa, which means wonderful, beautiful, supernatural law.

Sāgara. Dragon-King of the Ocean, whose palace is full of pearls, and who is the bestower of rain; p. 172.

Śakra, idem Indra.

Saha. A mortal world.

Śākyamuni. Saint of the Śākya clan, whose other names were Siddhārtha and Gautama.

Samādhi. Mystical meditation, concentrated contemplation, ecstatic absorption.

Saṃgha. The assembly of monks; the 'Church' of Buddhism, hence the third member of the trinity Buddha, Law, Church.

Sāriputra. Son of Śāri, the most learned of the Buddha's disciples.

Śramaṇa. A monk, an ascetic.

Śrāmaṇēras. Novices.

Śrāvaka. A hearer, or disciple; an elementary stage of sainthood.

Stūpa. A reliquary, or shrine, of cupola-shape to contain remains after cremation, especially of the Buddha.

Subhūti. One of the four oldest disciples; p. 129.

Sumēru. The central mountain of every world, whose height above the sea is 84,000 yōjanas, but whose total height from its invisible base to its summit is 168,000 yōjanas.

Sūtra. A work supposed to give the discourses of the Buddha.

Tāla. The fan palm; a length of about 70 feet.

Tathāgata. One who comes, or goes, as he should, a term for a Buddha.

Udumbara. A tree supposed to flower only once in 3,000 years.

Utpala. The blue lotus.

Vajra. The sceptre of Indra as god of lightning and thunder.

Vārāṇasī. Benares.

Yaksha. A class of demons.

Yōjana. A measure of length, a league, variously estimated at from 4½ to 9 miles.

INDEX

273

274